Crocheted Sweaters

SIMPLE STITCHES, GREAT DESIGNS

SUSAN HUXLEY

Martingale™
& COMPANY

Crocheted Sweaters: Simple Stitches, Great Designs
© 2001 by Susan Huxley

Martingale & Company
20205 144th Ave. NE
Woodinville, WA 98072-8478 USA
www.martingale-pub.com

Credits

President: **Nancy J. Martin**

CEO: **Daniel J. Martin**

Publisher: **Jane Hamada**

Editorial Director: **Mary V. Green**

Technical Editor: **Ursula Reikes**

Design and Production Manager: **Stan Green**

Illustrator: **Laurel Strand**

Produced by **Chris Rich**, Asheville, NC

Art Director: **Theresa Gwynn**

Photographer: **Brian Woodward**

Cover Photographer: **Brent Kane**

Printed in China
06 05 04 03 02 01   8 7 6 5 4 3 2 1

Library of Congress Cataloging-in-Publication Data available upon request.

ISBN: 1-56477-399-X

Mission Statement

We are dedicated to providing quality products and service by working together to inspire creativity and to enrich the lives we touch.

Dedication

To Ruth Gill,
my grandmother,
who taught
a squirmy little girl
to love the needle arts

Contents

Introduction

Welcome to *Crocheted Sweaters*. Even if you're a first-time visitor to the world of hooks and yarn, you'll soon be crocheting gorgeous garments for yourself, your family, and your friends. And if you're a seasoned pro who's tired of making stuffed animals and afghans, you've come to the right place.

When I decided to create this book, I had several goals in mind. First, I wanted to present a special collection of stylish, up-to-date crocheted garment designs—sweaters that beginners could make successfully but that didn't look as if they'd dropped out of cookie cutters. I've never believed that "easy to make" has to mean "boring." Some of today's top crochet designers very generously helped prove me right by contributing their outstanding work.

Newcomers to crochet often think that they can't stitch fashionable garments unless they know how to make fancy stitches. This just isn't true. Take a smattering of basic stitches, combine them in innovative ways, and the patterns that result can be astounding. And when those patterns are matched, as they are here, with classic shapes and lovely yarns, they can yield breathtakingly beautiful designs. The sweaters within these pages don't include complex patterns, and most are well within reach of beginners—even folks who've never held a crochet hook before.

I also wanted to offer beginners something I wish I'd had when I was learning to crochet—a one-stop guide to the basics. When I was five years old, my grandmother, Nannie Gill, scooped me up into her lap and taught me how to make a chain. After my family moved, and Nannie was no longer nearby, I learned most of the rest myself, bit by bit, from the illustrations in needlework and craft magazines. *Crocheted Sweaters* offers what those magazines couldn't: an illustrated introduction to basic stitches, a primer on how to read crochet instructions, guidance for perfecting fit, and more—all in one place.

Crocheting a first garment can be great fun, but I still remember how frustrated I was the first few times I tried. The only instructions I could find started out by telling me to make sure my stitches were the right size by stitching a small square of the featured pattern. How on earth was I supposed to figure out how to do this when the pattern instructions were buried in the sweater instructions? I'd have to make part of the sweater in order to make the swatch. I didn't, of course, and my first few garments fit—someone else!

I've tried to spare beginners this experience by providing separate pattern entries with every project. If you'd like to practice crocheting before you tackle a sweater, you can also use these patterns to make an afghan. Just browse through them, pick a few favorites, stitch some swatches that are all the same size, and sew the crocheted pieces together.

In no time at all, you'll be ready to make your first sweater. Finding one that fits won't be a problem. The instructions are written in an uncommonly wide range of sizes, from extra small to extra large. Whether your bust is 31½" or 43¼"—or anywhere in this range—you'll find instructions to match. Every set of instructions also includes design details, such as the sleeve and body length, the position of the shoulder seam, and whether the fit is loose or snug.

To advanced crocheters, this book offers a great collection of weekend projects and distinctive patterns. If you're handy with a hook, you may want to use one of the stitch patterns in a design of your own. You'll discover of wealth of professional tips and techniques, too, from instructions for making crocheted buttons and frogs to incorporating beads in stitches and weaving doubled yarn strands through finished fabric. Several sweaters are worked sideways, the sleeves of a few are made from shoulder to wrist, one has side panels, and another joins granny squares while making the last round of each piece.

As you read through the pages that follow, I hope you'll discover, as I have, that crocheting is a wonderfully relaxing and rewarding pastime. Just sit back, enjoy yourself—and fill your wardrobe with exclusive, handmade sweaters.

Crocheting Sensational Sweaters

What does it take to make this stunning selection of stylish sweaters? Surprisingly little. You don't have to know any fancy stitches, empty your savings account to buy yarn, or spend six weeks of your life with a hook in one hand, either. From casual cardigans to elegant vests, every one of the garments shown on these pages was designed with beginning crocheters, balanced budgets, and busy people in mind.

If you're a first-time crocheter, forget about spending two months practicing the stitches. You'll be ready to make your first sweater in a matter of days. Just start by reading the second part of this book, "All about Crochet." Then try out two simple stitches—the single and double crochet. As soon as you master them, you'll be ready for "Beginner's Luck," "Ins and Outs," and "Out of the Box" (see pages 8, 54, and 68). And once you've learned a few more basic stitches, every one of the special garments in this book can be yours.

Put away those tissues, too. The instructions were written to prevent tears of frustration. Every set includes a list of featured stitches and their abbreviations; a list of materials, including the yarn and hook size you'll need; a separate pattern entry, when a pattern is used, to make stitching a gauge swatch easy; row-by-row instructions, written for five sizes, all the way from extra small up to extra large; and at-a-glance schematics that define each garment's silhouette.

No matter which project takes your fancy—a warm winter pullover (see page 14); a summer-weight sleeveless shell with a matching beaded shawl (see page 28); or a casual hooded top (see page 72)—you'll soon be stitching exclusive sweaters that put ready-to-wear garments to shame.

Beginner's Luck

BY SUSAN HUXLEY

*T*his is the *sweater to try if you've never crocheted before—it's soft, cuddly, and so easy to make! The body and sleeves are worked in only one stitch (double crochet), and the yarn is thick enough to work with a big, fat hook. You'll be finished in no time at all.*

DESIGN DETAILS

- Loose fitting
- Body length to top of thighs
- Drop shoulder, three-quarter-length sleeve

FEATURED STITCHES

Chain (ch); see page 99

Double crochet (dc); see page 103

Single crochet (sc); see page 100

Slip stitch (sl st); see page 102

SIZING

To fit bust: 31½ (34¼, 37¼, 41, 43¼)"

Finished bust: 46½ (51, 55, 59, 61½)"

MATERIALS

6 (7, 8, 9, 9) skeins of Lion Brand *Chenille Thick & Quick* (91% acrylic, 9% rayon: 5 ozs./140 g; 94 yds./ 86 m); #136 Russett

P/16 (15 mm) crochet hook

6 stitch markers

GAUGE

6 dc to 4" and 4 rows to 4¾" in dc

NOTE: *Count the turning chain that starts each row as a stitch. At the start of each row, don't make a stitch into the stitch that the turning chain is built on. Instead, work into the next stitch. Remember to work the last double crochet of each row into the top of the turning chain in the previous row.* NOTE ALSO: *Schematics for this sweater are on page 10.*

Back

Ch 36 (40, 43, 46, 48).

Row 1: Dc in 4th ch from hook (count as dc) and in each ch to end, turn. [34 (38, 41, 44, 46) sts]

Row 2: Ch 3 (count as dc), dc in next and each st to end, turn.

Rep row 2 until 24¼ (25¼, 28¼, 29¼, 30¼)" from beg. Fasten off.

Place marker at both edges of work 17 (18, 19, 20, 21)" from beg.

Front

Work as for back.

Sleeve (Make 2)

Ch 22.

Row 1: Dc in 4th ch from hook (count as dc) and in each ch to end, turn. [20 sts]

Row 2: Ch 3 (count as dc), dc in first and each st across to last st, 2 dc in last st, turn. [22 sts]

Rep last 2 rows 0 (0, 3, 3, 3) more times. [22 (22, 28, 28, 28) dc]

Work even in dc until 13" from beg. Fasten off.

Finishing

At top of front, place marker 7¼ (8¼, 9¼, 10, 10½)" from each edge to mark inner edge of each shoulder. With RS tog, sew front to back at both shoulders.

Spread joined, opened front and back flat on a table, with RS facing you. Position sleeve across joined pieces, RS down, with wider end of sleeve between armhole markers on one side and aligned with edge of armhole. Sew sleeve to body. Attach rem sleeve in same manner.

Remove markers. Refold body and sleeves, RS in, aligning all matching edges. Join front and back by sewing up sides and along sleeve underarms.

NECK EDGING

Attach yarn at a shoulder seam. Sc in top of each st around neckline, join to first sc with sl st. Fasten off.

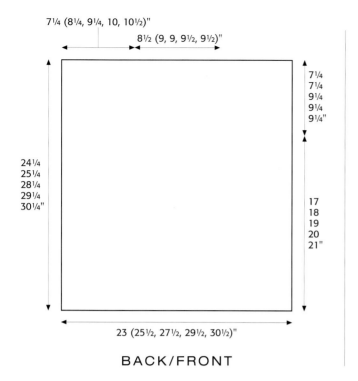

7¼ (8¼, 9¼, 10, 10½)"

8½ (9, 9, 9½, 9½)"

7¼
7¼
9¼
9¼
9¼"

24¼
25¼
28¼
29¼
30¼"

17
18
19
20
21"

23 (25½, 27½, 29½, 30½)"

BACK/FRONT

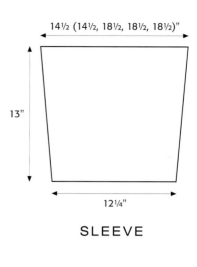

14½ (14½, 18½, 18½, 18½)"

13"

12¼"

SLEEVE

F O U N D A T I O N S

Fur, Chenille, and Similar Novelty Yarns

Stitches made with mohair, chenille, and other enticing, fluffy yarns can be difficult to see and therefore hard to work into and count. Ripping out your work when you've made a mistake can also be problematic with some of these yarns; the fibers that stick out from the core of the yarn strand tend to tangle into stubborn little knots.

Don't let these problems prevent you from making the fluffy sweaters in this book. All of the yarns have been carefully selected to make sure that they rip out easily. In addition, most of the patterns are set up so that you rarely have to find the top of a stitch. Instead, you make fabric that's full of holes, and work around the horizontal bars (chain-spaces) or between stitches. (Don't worry about the holes; fluffy yarns fill in all the gaps.)

Following are a few tips to help you make your fluffy sweater:

Go lightly. Place a light in front of you as you work. It will shine through the fabric and define the stitches, pattern repeats, and rows. To count stitches, pattern repeats, or rows, hold up the fabric so that light shines directly through it.

Be tipsy. As you work, keep the fabric slightly elevated and positioned at a bit of an angle.

Check yarn contents. Choose a yarn that's easy to rip out. Ones with nylon in them are often suitable. The yarn recommended for "Cat's Meow" (see page 36), for example, is 50 percent nylon.

Learn braille. Use your fingers to count stitches. To find the stitches in a base chain, for example, slide the stitches slowly between your thumb and forefinger. Each stitch starts with a nub or bump. Its center is smooth, and there's another bump at its end. (This last bump marks the end of one chain stitch and the beginning of the next.)

Cast away doubts. If working the first row into a base chain proves too difficult for you, either ask someone at your local yarn shop for help, or try this handy tip: make the base chain in a smooth yarn that's comparable to the sweater yarn in color and weight (or thickness). Fasten off. Next, use a slip stitch to attach the sweater yarn to the end of the chain. Then make the turning chain and begin the first row. This technique is used in "Lightning Strike" (see page 84).

Keep track. Make ample use of stitch markers to help you keep track of rows and pattern repeats within each row.

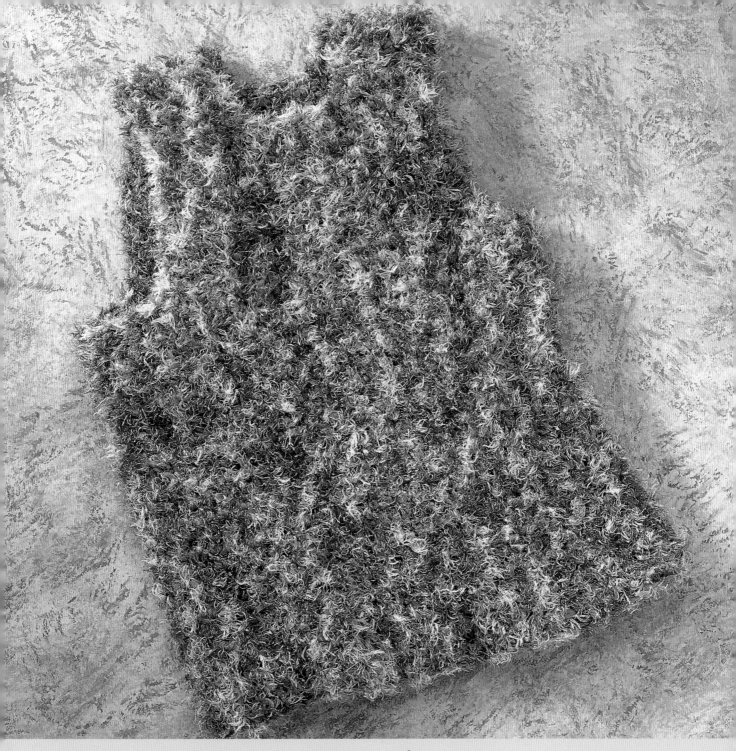

Snug Hug Tank Top

BY SUSAN HUXLEY

*U*sually, crocheted fabric has less stretch than knitted fabric, but the stretchy tulle core of this novelty yarn has just enough give to provide a snug fit. Don't worry, though: the yarn's fluffiness has the added benefit of camouflaging figure flaws! Choose a yarn color that flatters your face; the neckline of this tank sits above the collarbone, and its visual effect is similar to the one you'd get by wearing a scarf.

DESIGN DETAILS

- Body hugging
- Body length to high hip
- High jewel neckline ends above collarbone
- Shoulder straps angle slightly toward neck

FEATURED STITCHES

Chain (ch); see page 99

Chain-space (ch-sp); see page 111

Half double crochet (hdc); see page 103

Slip stitch (sl st); see page 102

SIZING

NOTE: *Your finished tank top should be smaller than your bust measurement; the crocheted fabric has built-in stretch that assures a perfect, snug fit.*

To fit bust: 31½ (34¼, 37¼, 41, 43¼)"

Finished bust: 28 (31, 34, 38, 40)"

MATERIALS

7 (7, 8, 9, 10) balls of Trendsetter *Dancer* (57% polyester, 43% polyamid: 1¾ ozs./50 g; 65 yds./59 m); #503 Purple Blossoms

M/13 (9 mm) crochet hook

GAUGE

NOTE: *Stretchy crocheted fabric distorts easily. Make sure the corners of the gauge swatch are square when you measure it.*

12 sts and 7 rows to 4" in Offset Filet pattern

OFFSET FILET PATTERN

Multiple of 2 sts (add 1 st for base chain)

Foundation Row: Hdc in 3rd ch from hook (count as 2 hdc), *ch 1, sk 1 ch, hdc in next ch*, rep from * to * to end, turn.

Row 1: Ch 2 (count as hdc), hdc around first ch-sp, *sk 1 st, ch 1, hdc around next ch-sp*, rep from * to * to end, working last hdc around tch, turn.

Rep row 1.

Back

Ch 43 (47, 51, 57, 61).

Row 1: As Offset Filet pat foundation row, turn. [42 (46, 50, 56, 60) sts]

Row 2: As pat row 1, turn.

Cont in pat until 13" from beg.

ARMHOLE SHAPING

Next Row: Sl st in first 7 (7, 9, 9, 11) sts (last sl st is in top of hdc), ch 2 (count as hdc), hdc around first ch-sp, *sk 1 st, ch 1, hdc around next ch-sp*, rep from * to * across to last 6 (6, 8, 8, 10) sts, turn. [30 (34, 34, 40, 40) sts]

Cont in pat until 16¼ (16¼, 16½, 17, 17)" from beg.

Next Row: Sl st in first 3 sts (worked in hdc, ch-sp and hdc), ch 2 (count as hdc), hdc around first ch-sp, *sk 1 st, ch 1, hdc around next ch-sp*, rep from * to * across to last 2 sts (hdc and tch), turn. Rem 2 sts unworked. [26 (30, 30, 36, 36) sts]

Large and Extra Large Only

Rep last row once. [32 sts]

All Sizes

Work even in pat until 18¼ (18¼, 18¾, 19¼, 19½)" from beg.

LEFT SHOULDER SHAPING

Next Row (Dec Row 1): Work in pat across 10 (12, 12, 12, 12) sts, turn. Rem 16 (18, 18, 24, 24) sts unworked.

Next Row (Dec Row 2): Sl st in first 2 sts (hdc and ch-sp), ch 2 (count as hdc), sk 1 hdc, hdc around next ch-sp, *sk 1 st, ch 1, hdc around next ch-sp*, rep from * to * to end, working last hdc around tch, turn. [8 (10, 10, 10, 10) sts]

Small and Medium Only

Next Row (Dec Row 3): Ch 2 (count as hdc), hdc around first ch-sp, *sk 1 st, ch 1, hdc around next ch-sp*, rep from * to * across to last 4 sts, ch 1, sk next (hdc, ch-sp, hdc), hdc around tch, turn. [8 sts]

All Sizes

Work 1 (1, 1, 2, 2) row even in pat. Fasten off.

RIGHT SHOULDER SHAPING

Next Row: Sk center 6 (6, 6, 8, 8) sts. Attach yarn with sl st in next hdc, work in pat to end, turn. [10 (12, 12, 12, 12) sts]

Next Row: As dec row 3 of left shoulder shaping, turn. [8 (10, 10, 10, 10) sts]

Small and Medium Only

Next Row: As dec row 2 of left shoulder shaping. [8 sts]

All Sizes

Work 1 (1, 1, 2, 2) row even in pat. Fasten off.

Front

Work as for back.

Finishing

With RS of front and back tog, sew shoulders and side seams.

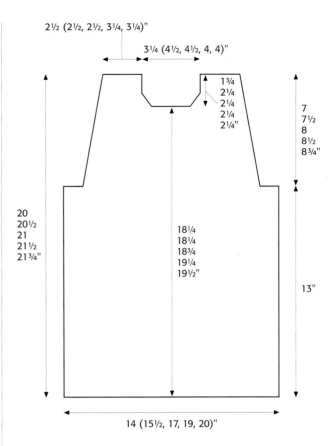

2½ (2½, 2½, 3¼, 3¼)"

3¼ (4½, 4½, 4, 4)"

1¾
2¼
2¼
2¼
2¼"

7
7½
8
8½
8¾"

20
20½
21
21½
21¾"

18¼
18¼
18¾
19¼
19½"

13"

14 (15½, 17, 19, 20)"

BACK/FRONT

Aran Classic

BY JANE SNEDDEN PEEVER

*T*he luxurious effect of a knitted, Aran-style sweater can be yours for the making, even
*if you don't know how to knit. The key component in this crocheted version, a group
of twisted stitches collectively called a cable stitch, can be challenging at first, especially
for beginners, so take your time and follow the instructions carefully.*

DESIGN DETAILS

- Loose fitting (very loose fitting in extra large)
- Drop shoulder and full-length sleeve
- Body length to below full hip

FEATURED STITCHES

3-stitch cable (cb3); see page 16

Chain (ch); see page 99

Double crochet (dc); see page 103

Front post double crochet (FPDC); see page 110

Single crochet (sc); see page 100

Single crochet 2 together (sc2tog); see page 111

SIZING

To fit bust: 31½ (34¼, 37¼, 41, 43¼)"

Finished bust: 40 (44, 48, 52, 57½)"

MATERIALS

8 (9, 9, 10, 11) balls of Patons *Decor* (75% acrylic, 25% wool: 3½ ozs./100 g; 210 yds./192 m); #1602 Aran

Size 7 (4.5 mm) crochet hook

H/8 (5 mm) crochet hook

2 stitch markers

GAUGE

14 sts and 13 rows to 4" in Crumpled Griddle Stitch variation, with H/8 (5 mm) hook

NOTE: *For all patterns in this sweater, don't count the ch-1 turning chain at the start of a row as a stitch. In other words, work the first single crochet into the first stitch of the previous row. At the end of the row, don't make the last stitch into the turning chain.*

CRUMPLED GRIDDLE STITCH VARIATION

Multiple of 2 sts + 1 st (also add 1 st for base chain)

Foundation Row (RS): Sc in 2nd ch from hook, dc in next ch, *sc in next ch, dc in next ch*, rep from * to * across to last st, sc in last st, turn.

Row 1 (WS): Ch 1, sc in first and each st to end, turn.

Row 2: Ch 1, *sc in first st, dc in next st*, rep from * to * across to last st, sc in last st, turn.

Rep rows 1 and 2.

LEFT CROSS CABLE PATTERN

NOTE: *This pattern includes a 3-stitch cable (cb3), instructions for which are provided in "Crocheted Cables" on page 16. The cb3 in this pattern is sandwiched between 2 vertical FPDC posts.*

Multiple of 10 sts + 6 sts (also add 1 st for base chain)

Foundation Row (RS): Sc in 2nd ch from hook and in each ch to end, turn.

Row 1 (WS): Ch 1, sc in each st to end, turn.

Row 2 (RS): Ch 1, *sc in each of first 3 sts, FPDC around next st in row below (at beg of row, this is 4th st from start), sk 1 st in previous row (behind FPDC just made), sc in each of next 3 sts, cb3, sk 3 sts in previous row (behind FPDCs just made)*, rep from * to * across to last 6 sts, sc in each of next 3 sts, FPDC in row below around 4th st from cb3 just worked, sk 1 st in previous row (behind FPDC just worked), sc in each of next 2 sts, turn.

Rows 3, 5, and 7 (WS): Ch 1, sc in first and each st to end, turn.

Row 4 (RS): Ch 1, *sc in each of first 3 sts, FPDC around FPDC in row below, sk 1 st in previous row, sc in each of next 3 sts, FPDC around each of first 2 FPDC of cb3 in row below, FPDC around 3rd FPDC (the one on top) in row below, sk 3 sts in previous row*, rep from * to * to last 6 sts, sc in each of next 3 sts, FPDC around FPDC in row below, sk 1 st in previous row (behind FPDC just worked), sc in each of next 2 sts, turn.

Row 6 (RS): Ch 1, *sc in each of first 3 sts, FPDC around FPDC in row below, sk 1 st in previous row, sc in each of next 3 sts, cb3 (work each new FPDC around FPDC in row below), sk 3 sts in previous row*, rep from * to * across to last 6 sts, sc in each of next 3 sts, FPDC around next FPDC in row below, sk 1 st in previous row (behind FPDC just worked), sc in each of next 2 sts, turn.

Rep rows 3–6.

Back

With size 7 (4.5 mm) hook, ch 70 (78, 86, 94, 102).

CABLE RIBBING

NOTE: *This is a slight variation of the Left Cross Cable pattern. In row 2, there are 2 single crochets, not 3, between each FPDC and cb3. In addition, only rows 2 and 3 of the Left Cross Cable pattern are repeated.*

Row 1 (RS): Sc in 2nd ch from hook and in each ch across, turn. [69 (77, 85, 93, 101) sts]

Row 2 (WS): Ch 1, sc in first and each st to end, turn.

Row 3: Ch 1, sc in each of first 2 sts, FPDC around 3rd st from start in row below, sk 1 st in previous row (behind FPDC just made), sc in each of next 2 sts, cb3 (work around 4th and 5th sts from FPDC just made in row below), sk 3 sts in previous row (behind FPDCs just made), *sc in next 2 sts, FPDC in row below (around 3rd st from cb3 just worked), sk 1 st in previous row, sc in each of next 2 sts, cb3, sk 3 sts in previous row (behind FPDC just made)*, rep from * to * across to last 5 sts, sc in each of next 2 sts, FPDC

F O U N D A T I O N S

CROCHETED CABLES

Many crocheters long to create sophisticated knitted effects in their work, but they have trouble finding instructions. Well, here's a gorgeous cable pattern that's actually not as difficult to achieve as it might look at first glance. As soon as you've mastered the front post double crochet (FPDC) on page 110, you'll be ready to tackle the 3-stitch cable (cb3) that's featured in this sweater.

Made with double-crochet stitches worked into the row below, this is a left cross cable. In other words, the twist starts at the lower right and travels toward the upper left. You set up the stitch by working two rows of single crochet. In the row in which you work the cables, you make several single-crochet stitches between each cable. The effect emerges two rows later, when you work groups of uncrossed FPDC to complete the cable pattern.

To make the cb3 in the pattern, you start by skipping a stitch. Then you work an FPDC into each of the next two stitches of the row below. Next, you backtrack to the skipped stitch to make the final FPDC and create the crossed effect.

Following is the step-by-step process for making a cb3:

1. Skip the first stitch.

2. YO, and insert the hook into the work, from front to back, between the first and second stitch from the hook, in the row below.

3. Insert the hook through the work, from back to front, between the second and third stitch in the row below.

4. YO, and pull the loop through the work from front to back to front.

5. Complete the stitch following steps 3 and 4 of "Double Crochet" on page 103. (One FPDC made in the row below.)

6. Make another FPDC around the next stitch in the row below by following steps 2–5 above.

7. Make an FPDC in the row below, around the post of the skipped stitch. Do this by working across the front of the 2 completed FPDCs.

The next row is all single crochet, and then, in the row after that, you work 3 uncrossed FPDCs to complete the pattern repeat. In subsequent rows, work each FPDC around the FPDC in the row below.

in row below around 3rd st from cb3 just worked, sk 1 st in previous row (behind FPDC just worked), sc in each of next 2 sts, turn.

Rep rows 2 and 3 until 3" from beg, ending with RS row completed.

BODY

Change to H/8 (5 mm) hook.

Next Row (WS): As row 2 of Crumpled Griddle St var, turn.

Next Row: As row 1 of Crumpled Griddle St var, turn.

Cont in pat as established until 25 (26, 26, 27, 29)" from beg. Fasten off.

Front

Work as for back until 22 (23, 23, 24, 26)" from beg, ending with RS completed.

LEFT SHOULDER SHAPING

Next Row (WS): Ch 1, sc in first 27 (31, 35, 39, 43) sts, turn. Rem 42 (46, 50, 54, 58) sts unworked.

Next Row: As row 2 of Crumpled Griddle St var, turn.

Next Row: Ch 1, sc in first and each st across to last 5 sts, sc2tog twice, sc in last st, turn. [25 (29, 33, 37, 41) sts]

Rep last 2 rows 2 more times. [21 (25, 29, 33, 37) sts]

Work even in pat until 25 (26, 26, 27, 29)" from beg. Fasten off.

RIGHT SHOULDER SHAPING

Next Row (WS): Working on last full row, sk center 15 sts (counting from neckline st at base of left shoulder), attach yarn with sc in next st, sc in next and each st to end, turn. [27 (31, 35, 39, 43) sts]

Next Row: As row 2 of Crumpled Griddle St var, turn.

Next Row: Ch 1, sc in first st, sc2tog twice, sc in next and each st to end, turn. [25 (29, 33, 37, 41) sts]

Rep last 2 rows 2 more times. [21 (25, 29, 33, 37) sts]

Work even in pat until 25 (26, 26, 27, 29)" from beg. Fasten off.

Sleeve (Make 2)

With size 7 (4.5 mm) hook, ch 30.

CABLE RIBBING

Work as for back cable ribbing until 3" from beg, ending with RS row completed. [29 sts]

Next Row (WS): Ch 1, sc in first 4 sts, 2 sc in next st, *sc in next 3 sts, 2 sc in next st*, rep from * to * to end, turn. [36 sts]

ARM

Change to H/8 (5 mm) hook.

Work rows 6, 3, 4, 5, and 6 of Left Cross Cable pat.

Next Row (Row 3 of Left Cross Cable Pat): Ch 1, 2 sc in first st (inc made), sc in next and each st across to last st, 2 sc in last st (inc made), turn. [38 sts]

Cont in pat as established (work row 4 next), AT SAME TIME inc 1 st at beg and end of every row 3 of Left Cross Cable pat 6 more times. (Work sc into new sts.) [50 sts]

Rep rows 4 and 5 of Left Cross Cable pat once.

Next Row: Ch 1, sc in each of first 4 sts, cb3 (work each new FPDC around sc in row below), sk 3 sts in previous row, work in pat as established to last 3 sts, sc in last 3 sts, turn.

Cont in pat as established (work row 4 next), AT SAME TIME inc 1 st at beg and end of every row 3 of Left Cross Cable pat 6 more times. [62 sts]

Work even in pat as established until 18" from beg. Fasten off.

Collar

With RS tog, sew front to back at right shoulder.

Using size 7 (4.5 mm) crochet hook, attach yarn to front at neckline of left shoulder.

Row 1 (RS): Work 10 sc along left side of neck, 15 sc across front, 10 sc up right side of neck, and 29 sc across neckline on back, turn. [64 sts]

Row 2: Ch 1, sc in first and each st to end, turn.

Row 3: As row 3 of cable ribbing for back, working pat reps (from * to *) across to last 8 sts, work 1 more rep to end, turn.

Row 4: Ch 1, sc in first and each st to end of row, turn.

Rep last 2 rows until 4" from beg. Fasten off.

Finishing

With RS tog, sew front to back at left shoulder and collar.

Spread joined, opened front and back flat on a table, with RS facing you. Place markers along one side, each 10" from a shoulder seam, to mark armhole. Position sleeve across joined pieces, RS down, with wider end between markers and aligned with edge of armhole. Sew sleeve to body. Remove markers. Attach rem sleeve in same manner.

Refold body and sleeves, RS tog, aligning all matching edges. Join front and back by sewing up sides and along sleeve underarms.

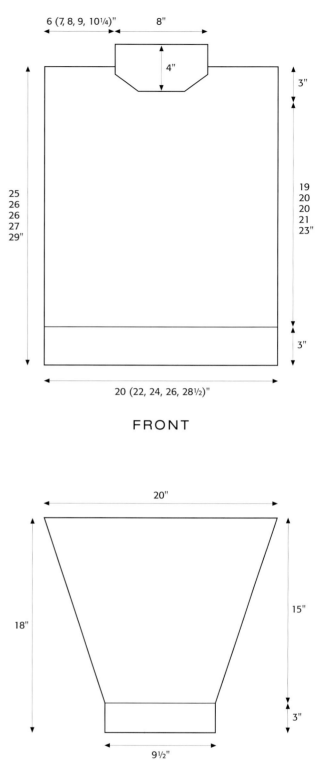

FRONT

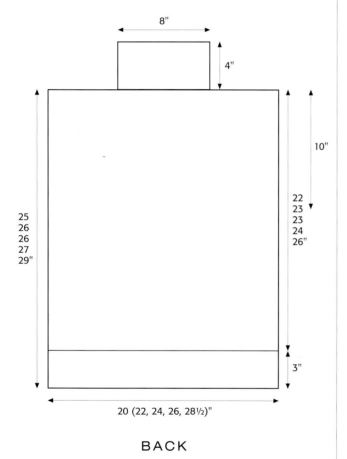

BACK

SLEEVE

Double Stripes

BY TRICIA CRICHTON

*S*lip *into casual weekend mode with this chic and comfortable oversize sweater. Its subtle checkerboard effect is created by stitching rows of alternating colors. The sleeves are stitched at the same time as the body, and the yokes are stitched onto the front and back after the garment pieces are partly assembled.*

DESIGN DETAILS

- Very loose fitting
- Round neck
- Full-length dolman sleeve
- Body length to just above high hip

FEATURED STITCHES

Chain (ch); see page 99

Chain-space (ch-sp); see page 111

Single crochet (sc); see page 100

Single crochet 2 together (sc2tog); see page 111

Slip stitch (sl st); see page 102

SIZING

To fit bust: 31½ (34¼, 37¼, 41, 43¼)"

Finished bust: 41 (45, 50½, 53½, 57½)"

MATERIALS

Berroco *Cotton Twist* (70% mercerized cotton, 30% rayon: 1¾ ozs./50 g; 85 yds./77 m): 9 (9, 9, 9, 10) hanks of #8363 Emerald Isle (MC); and 9 (9, 10, 10, 12) hanks of #8319 Periwinkle Blue (A)

G/6 (4.25 mm) crochet hook

4 stitch markers

NOTE: *Working directly from a hank is asking for trouble, so wind each one into a ball before you start stitching.*

GAUGE

25 sts and 24 rows to 5" in Offset Single Crochet pattern

OFFSET SINGLE CROCHET PATTERN

NOTE: *Don't count the ch-1 turning chain at the start of the row as a stitch. Work the first stitch in the new row into the first stitch of the previous row. At the end of the row, don't work into the turning chain of the previous row.*

Multiple of 2 sts (add 1 st for base chain)

Foundation Row: Sc in 2nd ch from hook, ch 1, sk next ch, *sc, ch 1, sk next ch*, rep from * to * to last 2 chs, sc in each of last 2 chs, turn.

Row 1: Ch 1, sc in first sc, ch 1, sk next sc, *sc around next ch-sp, ch 1, sk next sc*, rep from * to * to last 2 sts, sc in each of last 2 sts, turn.

Rep row 1.

WORKING IN PATTERN DURING AND AFTER SHAPING

This is a simple pattern, but decreases can throw off the repeat at the beginning and end of a row. The solution is easy: maintain the established pattern across the row by adjusting the first or last 2 stitches. Here's how:

1. Start and end each row with a single crochet, even if the second stitch from the end is a single crochet.
2. The second stitch at the start of the row you're making is a single crochet if the next stitch in the previous row is a chain.
3. The second stitch at the start of the row you're making is a chain if the next stitch in the previous row is a single crochet.

COLOR PATTERN

Change yarn colors at the end of a row. Start each garment piece with the MC; then alternate with A in the following manner:

First 1½" from Beg: Change color every other row. Carry yarn not in use along edge of work.

***Next 3":** Change color every row by cutting one color and joining the next.

Next 3": Change color every other row.*

Rep from * to * to end of work.

Back Sleeves and Body

With MC, ch 297 (301, 305, 313, 325).

Row 1: As pat foundation row, turn. [296 (300, 304, 312, 324) sts]

Row 2: As pat row 1. Join A, turn.

Work even in pat for 20 (20, 22, 23, 25) rows, AT SAME TIME stop using A at end of third row. Pick up MC, which is hanging unworked at the side, cont working even in pat, alternating between MC and A every other row until 1½" from beg of work. Then foll color pat as you work rem rows (including lower sleeve and body shaping) to end of back.

LOWER SLEEVE SHAPING

Next Row: Sl st in first 6 (6, 9, 8, 7) sts, sc in next st, work across in pat to last 7 (7, 10, 9, 8) sts, sc in next st, turn. Rem 6 (6, 9, 8, 7) sts unworked. [284 (288, 286, 296, 310) sts]

Rep last row 7 (7, 4, 6, 7) more times. Fasten off. Turn. [200 (204, 214, 200, 212) sts]

BODY SHAPING

Next Row: Join yarn with sc in 23rd (22nd, 13th, 10th, 9th) st from beg, work in pat across to last 23 (22, 13, 10, 9) sts, sc in next st. Fasten off. Turn. [156 (162, 190, 182, 196) sts]

Rep last row 1 (1, 2, 2, 3) more time. Don't fasten off last row unless you're changing colors. [112 (120, 142, 146, 148) sts]

Next Row: Sl st in first 5 (4, 8, 6, 2) sts, sc in next st, work in pat across to last 6 (5, 9, 7, 3) sts, sc in next st, turn. Rem 5 (4, 8, 6, 2) sts unworked. [102 (112, 126, 134, 144) sts]

Rep last row 0 (0, 0, 0, 3) more times. [102 (112, 126, 134, 132) sts]

X-Small, Small, Medium, and Large Only

Next Row: Sl st in first 2 sts, sc in next st, work in pat across to last 3 sts, sc in next st, turn. Rem 2 sts unworked. [98 (108, 122, 130) sts]

Rep last row 1 (1, 2, 1) more time. [94 (104, 114, 126) sts]

All Sizes

Next Row: Ch 1, sc2tog over first 2 sts, work in pat across to last 2 sts, sc2tog, turn. [92 (102, 112, 124, 130) sts]

Rep last row 0 (0, 2, 0, 0) more times. [92 (102, 108, 124, 130) sts]

Work even in pat until 82 (83, 84, 87, 94) rows completed. Fasten off.

Right Front

With MC, ch 133 (135, 137, 141, 143).

SLEEVE AND NECKLINE SHAPING

Row 1: As pat foundation row, turn. [132 (134, 136, 140, 142) sts]

Place marker anywhere along row 1 to indicate RS.

Row 2: Ch 3, sc in 2nd ch from hook (neck edge inc made), ch 1, sk next sc, sc in next sc, ch 1, sk next sc, *sc around next ch-sp, ch 1, sk next sc*, rep from * to * to last 2 sts, sc in each of last 2 sts. Fasten off. Join A, turn. [134 (136, 138, 142, 144) sts]

Row 3: Work in pat to last 2 sts, sc around next ch-sp, ch 1, 2 sc in last sc (neck inc made). [136 (138, 140, 144, 146) sts]

Rep last 2 rows 1 (1, 2, 3, 5) more time. [140 (142, 146, 150, 158) sts]

AT SAME TIME alternate between MC and A until 1½" from beg of work. Then foll color pat as you work rem rows for right front.

Rep row 2 for 1 (1, 1, 1, 0) more time. [142 (144, 148, 152, 158) sts]

Place marker in last st worked on neck edge. Fasten off.

Left Front

Work as for right front to end of sleeve and neckline shaping, EXCEPT place marker on row 2 to mark the RS. Don't fasten off.

Ch 13 (13, 9, 11, 9). Make sure the chain isn't twisted; then join with sl st in st with marker at end of row on right front. Fasten off.

SLEEVES AND UPPER BODY

Next Row; Right Sleeve and Body: Join yarn with sc in first st of cuff edge of right front, work across in pat to last 2 sts before marker, ch 1, sk next sc, sc in st with marker (already has sl st in it), remove marker, and cont with neckline.

Neckline: Ch 1, sk 1 ch, *sc in next ch, cont working in pat across ch to marker, and cont with left body and sleeve.

Left Body and Sleeve: Sc in st with marker, cont working in pat to end of row. Remove markers in previous row. Turn. [297 (301, 305, 315, 325) sts]

Work even in pat for 14 (14, 15, 16, 16) more rows.

LOWER SLEEVE SHAPING

As lower sleeve shaping for back. [201 (205, 215, 201, 213) sts]

BODY SHAPING

As body shaping for back. [93 (103, 109, 125, 131) sts]

Yoke Preparation

At upper edge of back, place marker in 112th (114th, 116th, 116th, 120th, 122nd) st from beg of both sleeves.

With RS tog, sew front to back at upper edge, from cuff to marker on both sides. Don't seam center 72 (72, 72, 72, 80) sts.

Back Yoke

Cont alternating MC and A as established, and work foll rows across back only between markers at shoulder seams.

Use sl st to join yarn to back neckline at marker.

Row 1: Ch 1, sk first st, sc2tog over next 2 sts, work in pat to last 3 sts, sc2tog over last 2 sts, turn. Rem st unworked. [68 (68, 68, 68, 76) sts]

Rep last row 5 more times. Fasten off. [48 (48, 48, 48, 56) sts]

Front Yoke (Make 2)

Cont alternating MC and A as established.

Use sl st to join yarn to front neckline at marker.

Row 1: Sc2tog over first 2 sts, work in pat to last 2 sts, sc2tog over last 2 sts, turn. [17 sts]

Row 2: Ch 1, sk first st, sc2tog over next 2 sts, work in pat to last 2 sts, sc2tog over last 2 sts, turn. [14 sts]

Row 3: Ch 1, sc2tog over first 2 sts, work in pat to last 3 sts, sc2tog over next 2 sts, turn. Rem st unworked. [11 sts]

Row 4: Ch 1, sc2tog over first 2 sts, work in pat to last 3 sts, sc2tog over next 2 sts, turn. Rem st unworked. [8 sts]

Row 5: As row 4. [5 sts]

Row 6: Ch 1, sc2tog over next 2 sts twice. Rem st unworked. Fasten off, leaving a long yarn strand to sew shoulder seam. [2 sts]

Finishing

Remove markers. With RS tog, sew front to back at side and underarm seams. Sew front yokes to back yoke.

HEM EDGING

Rnd 1: Join MC with sc around ch-sp near side seam, work in pat around hem edge, sl st in first sc of rnd to join beg and end of rnd.

Rnd 2: Sl st in first st, ch 1, work in pat to end of rnd and finishing with a ch 1, join to first ch 1 with sl st.

CUFF EDGING

Rnd 1: Join MC near underarm seam at wrist with sc in row that ended with a sc, work in pat around cuff by making ch 1 over rows that end with 2 sc, skipping those rows, and placing sc in rows ending with 1 sc; then sl st in first sc of rnd to join beg and end of rnd. Make cuff for rem sleeve in same manner.

NECKLINE EDGING

Rnd 1: Use sc to join MC near shoulder seam, work in pat around front and back neck, sl st in first sc of rnd to join beg and end of rnd.

Rnd 2: Sl st in first st, ch 1, work in pat to end of rnd and finishing with a ch 1, join to first ch 1 with sl st.

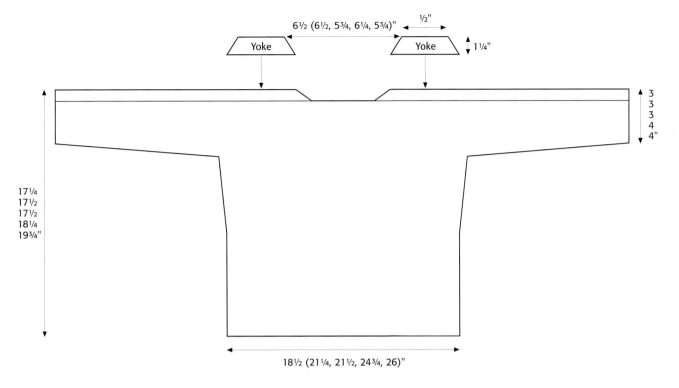

6½ (6½, 5¾, 6¼, 5¾)" ½"

Yoke   Yoke   1¼"

3
3
3
4
4"

17¼
17½
17½
18¼
19¾"

18½ (21¼, 21½, 24¾, 26)"

FRONT

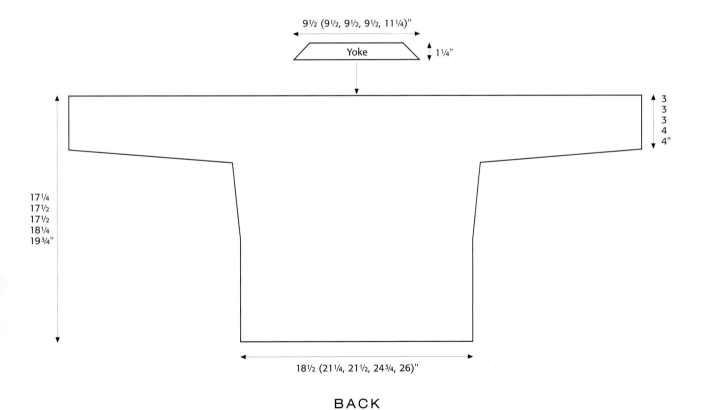

9½ (9½, 9½, 9½, 11¼)"

Yoke   1¼"

3
3
3
4
4"

17¼
17½
17½
18¼
19¾"

18½ (21¼, 21½, 24¾, 26)"

BACK

Two-Way Tee

BY JANET REHFELDT

*Y*ou can't beat this cropped, cap sleeve T-shirt sweater for a casual day at the office. Its ingenious reversible design features a round neckline on one side and a squared neckline on the other. (Choice is a wonderful thing, isn't it?) And the lovely Textured Lace pattern is Janet's own invention.

DESIGN DETAILS

- Loose, boxy fit
- Body length to high hip
- Cap sleeve worked as part of the yoke
- Bottom half worked vertically (side to side)
- Yoke stitched horizontally by working into edge of sweater body

FEATURED STITCHES

Chain (ch); see page 99

Extended single crochet (esc); see page 105

Half double crochet (hdc); see page 103

Reverse single crochet (rsc); see page 104

Single crochet (sc); see page 100

Single crochet 2 together (sc2tog); see page 111

Slip stitch (sl st); see page 102

SIZING

To fit bust: 31½ (34¼, 37¼, 41, 43¼)"

Finished bust: 37½ (40½, 43½, 47, 49½)"

MATERIALS

4 (5, 5, 6, 6) skeins of Brown Sheep *Cotton Fleece* (80% cotton, 20% merino wool: 3½ ozs./100 g; 215 yds./ 196 m); #CW-490 Fermi Green

Size 7 (4.5 mm) crochet hook

E/4 (3.5 mm) crochet hook

GAUGE

15 sts and 14 rows to 4" in Textured Lace pattern, with size 7 (4.5 mm) hook

15 sts and 24 rows to 4" in Seed Stitch pattern, with size 7 (4.5 mm) hook

TEXTURED LACE PATTERN

NOTE: *Don't count the turning chain as a stitch or work into it unless told to do so.*

Multiple of 2 sts (add 1 st for base chain)

Foundation Row (RS): Sc in 2nd ch from hook and in each st to end, turn.

Row 1: Ch 1, esc in first and each st to end, turn.

Row 2: Ch 1, sc in first and each st to end, turn.

Row 3: Ch 1, hdc in first sc, *sk one sc, hdc in next sc, hdc in skipped sc*, rep from * to * to last sc, hdc in last sc, turn.

Row 4: Ch 1, sc in next and each st to end, turn.

Rep rows 1–4.

SEED STITCH PATTERN

NOTE: *Be sure not to work the slip stitches tightly, and don't work into the turning chain unless told to do so.*

Multiple of 2 sts + 1 (also add 1 st for base chain)

Foundation Row: Sc in 2nd ch from hook and in each ch to end, turn.

Row 1: Ch 1, *sc in first st, sl st in next st*, rep from * to * across to last st, sc in last st, turn.

Row 2: Ch 1, sl st in each sc, sc in each sl st to end, turn.

Rep row 2.

NOTE: *Because this sweater is reversible, "front" and "back" are called "side 1" and "side 2." Each side consists of a body (the section below the bust) and a yoke (the portion from the bust to the shoulders). The outer edges of the yoke extend beyond the shoulders to act as cap sleeves.* **NOTE ALSO:** *The rows of each body section run vertically in the sweater. As you make each side piece, when the body is wide enough to fit you, you pivot the piece 90° and make the first row of the horizontal yoke by stitching along one edge of the body.*

Side 1 (Round Neckline)

With size 7 (4.5 mm) hook, ch 37 (39, 41, 43, 45).

Row 1 (RS): Sc in 2nd ch from hook, sc in next and each ch to end, turn. [36 (38, 40, 42, 44) sts]

Rep Textured Lace pat rows 1–4 until 18¾ (20½, 21¾, 23½, 24½)" from beg, ending with RS completed. Don't turn.

YOKE AND SLEEVE SHAPING

Row 1 (RS): Ch 2 loosely, sc in the bottom lp of each of the 2 ch sts just made. Pivot sweater and work 66 (70, 74, 80, 86) sc evenly spaced across the side edge of the piece to last sc (don't work into edge st of last row), insert hook into edge st of last row, YO, pull up lp, YO, pull through 1 lp on hook (ch made), YO, pull through 2 lps on hook, *insert hook into ch made at base of sc just finished, YO, pull up lp, YO, pull through 1 lp on hook (ch made), YO, pull through 2 lps on hook*, rep from * to * 1 more time, turn. [70 (74, 78, 84, 90) sts]

Row 2 (Seed Stitch Pat): Ch 1, (sc, sl st) in first st, *sc in next sc, sl st in next sc*, rep from * to * to last st, (sc, sl st) in last sc, turn. [72 (76, 80, 86, 92) sts]

Row 3: Ch 1, (sl st, sc) in first st, *sl st in next sc, sc in next sl st*, rep from * to * to last st, (sl st, sc) in last st, turn. [74 (78, 82, 88, 94) sts]

Row 4: Ch 1, sl st in first st, sc in next st, *sl st in next sc, sc in next sl st*, rep from * to * to end, turn.

Work even in Seed St pat as established, working sl st in each sc of the previous row and sc in each sl st, until 5 (5½, 6, 6½, 7)" from beg of yoke and sleeve shaping. End with RS row completed.

RIGHT SHOULDER SHAPING (ROUND NECKLINE)

Next Row (WS): Work across 30 (32, 34, 36, 38) sts in Seed St pat as established, turn. Rem 44 (46, 48, 52, 56) sts unworked.

Next Row (Dec Row): Ch 1, sc2tog, work in pat to end, turn. [29 (31, 33, 35, 37) sts]

Cont in Seed St pat, dec 1 st at neck edge (sc2tog) 3 more times. [26 (28, 30, 32, 34) sts]

Cont in Seed St pat, dec 1 st at neck edge every other row to 22 (24, 26, 28, 30) sts.

Work even in Seed St pat until 18 (19, 20, 21, 22)" from beg. Fasten off.

LEFT SHOULDER SHAPING (ROUND NECKLINE)

Next Row (WS): From the inner (neckline) edge of first row of right shoulder, sk center 14 (14, 14, 16, 18) sts, attach yarn in next st with sl st, ch 1, work to end in Seed St pat as established, turn. [30 (32, 34, 36, 38) sts]

Work as right shoulder shaping, dec 1 st at neck edge every row 4 times, then every other row 4 times. [22 (24, 26, 28, 30) sts]

Work even to match right shoulder. Fasten off.

Side 2 (Square Neckline)

Work as for side 1 to right shoulder shaping.

RIGHT SHOULDER SHAPING (SQUARE NECKLINE)

Next Row (WS): Work across 22 (24, 26, 28, 30) sts in Seed St pat as established, turn.

Cont in pat until 9 (9½, 10, 10½, 11)" from beg of yoke and sleeve shaping. Fasten off.

LEFT SHOULDER SHAPING (SQUARE NECKLINE)

Next Row (WS): From the inner (neckline) edge of first row of right shoulder, sk center 30 (30, 30, 32, 34) sts. Attach yarn in next st with sl st, ch 1, work in pat as established to end, turn. [22 (24, 26, 28, 30) sts]

Cont in pat until same length as right shoulder. Fasten off.

Finishing

Block garment pieces.
With RS of side 1 and side 2 tog, sew shoulder and side seams.

NECK EDGING

With E/4 (3.5 mm) hook and RS facing you, attach yarn at shoulder.

Rnd 1 (RS): Ch 1, work 128 (132, 136, 142, 148) evenly spaced sc around neckline, making 2 sc at both inner (square) corners on side 2, sl st in first sc to join beg and end of rnd.

Rnd 2: Ch 1, sc in first and each sc to end, working sc2tog over 2 sts at each inner corner of square neckline only, sl st in first sc to join beg and end of rnd.

Rnd 3: Ch 1, rsc in first and each sc around neckline, working rsc2tog over 2 sts in inner corners of square neckline only. Fasten off.

SLEEVE EDGING

With E/4 (3.5 mm) hook and RS facing you, attach yarn at one underarm.

Rnd 1: Ch 1, work 62 (64, 68, 72, 76) evenly spaced sc around sleeve opening, sl st in first sc to join beg and end of rnd.

Rnds 2 and 3: Ch 1, sc in first and each sc around, sl st in first sc to join beg and end of rnd.

Rnd 4: Ch 1, rsc in first and each sc around. Fasten off.

Rep for rem sleeve.

BOTTOM EDGING

With E/4 (3.5 mm) hook and RS facing you, attach yarn at side edge.

Rnd 1: Work 134 (142, 150, 162, 174) evenly spaced sc around bottom of sweater, sl st in first sc to join beg and end of rnd.

Rnds 2 and 3: Ch 1, sc in first and each sc around, sl st in first sc to join beg and end of rnd. Fasten off.

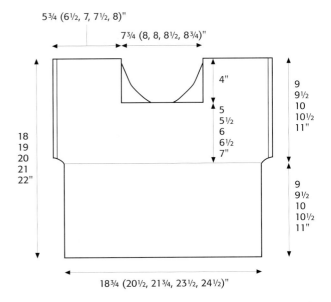

5¾ (6½, 7, 7½, 8)"

7¾ (8, 8, 8½, 8¾)"

4"

5
5½
6
6½
7"

9
9½
10
10½
11"

18
19
20
21
22"

9
9½
10
10½
11"

18¾ (20½, 21¾, 23½, 24½)"

SIDE 1/SIDE 2

F O U N D A T I O N S
ON THE EDGE

Like the icing on a cake, an edging gives your sweater a finished look. Positioned at the neckline, cuffs, and/or hem, an edging can consist of a single row of simple stitches or multiple rounds of a complex lace pattern. Its characteristics depend on the type of yarn, the designer's vision for the finished garment, the edging's function, and the way in which the sweater pieces are joined.

A deep, lace-like edging, for example, looks great worked in a smooth fiber. The yarn for "Two-Way Tee" is suitable for this type of edging, yet designer Janet Rehfeldt chose to create two rounds of single crochet. This was an excellent decision. Her edging reinforces the sweater's casual style, and it doesn't draw attention away from the attractive Textured Lace pattern featured on the lower half of the body. In this sweater, the edging also serves a functional purpose: it controls stretch at the neckline, cuffs, and hem.

In order to add the edging, Janet first asks you to make the garment pieces. Only after they're finished and joined do you attach the yarn and start the rounds for the edging. On occasion, an edging may be stitched in rows.

Some sweaters don't have edgings. "Beginner's Luck" (see page 8) is a good example. Chenille, the type of yarn used to make this sweater, is so fluffy that a small edging wouldn't be visible. Moreover, chenille—and the stitch used for the sweater—are relatively firm, so it's unlikely that the edges will stretch much. Even if they do, this just adds to the casual charm of the sweater styling.

Edgings provide a wonderful opportunity to add a complex or interesting pattern or stitch to a sweater. Even if you have only a little stitching experience, you'll probably be skilled enough to substitute an edging of your choice for one that's specified in a pattern. Entire books are dedicated to edging stitches and patterns, so you're sure to find plenty of inspiration.

Evening Shade

BY ANNABELLE DAWSON

*T*he iridescent beads in this elegant matching shell and stole capture all the magic of a special night on the town. They're easy to add, too. You simply thread them onto your yarn before you start to crochet and pull them up, one by one, as you work. You'll also love handling the yarn itself; it's exquisitely smooth.

DESIGN DETAILS

- Close fitting
- Body length to slightly below high hip
- Front neckline rests on collarbone

FEATURED STITCHES

Chain (ch); see page 99

Chain-space (ch-sp); see page 111

Double crochet (dc); see page 103

Half double crochet (hdc); see page 103

Reverse single crochet (rsc); see page 104

Single crochet (sc); see page 100

Slip stitch (sl st); see page 102

SIZING

To fit bust: 31½ (34¼, 37¼, 41, 43¼)"

Finished bust: 35 (38, 41, 44½, 47½)"

Stole: 11" x 61"

MATERIALS

Shell: 6 (7, 8, 9, 10) balls of Filatura Di Crosa *Millefilli Fine* (100% cotton: 1¾ ozs./50 g; 136½ yds./123 m); #180 Ultramarine

Stole: 3 balls of Filatura Di Crosa *Millefilli Fine* (100% cotton: 1¾ ozs./50 g; 136½ yds./123 m); #180 Ultramarine

C/2 (3 mm) crochet hook (for shell)

E/4 (3.5 mm) crochet hook (for shell)

H/8 (5 mm) crochet hook (for stole)

3 ozs. (90 ml) of #5 iridescent seed beads

Fine beading wire, 6" (15 cm) long

1 stitch marker

GAUGE

31 sts and 20 rows to 5" in Offset Filet pattern, with E/4 (3.5 mm) hook

OFFSET FILET PATTERN

Multiple of 2 sts (add 1 st for base chain)

Foundation Row: Hdc in 3rd ch from hook (count tch as hdc), *ch 1, sk 1 st, hdc in next st (tch)*, rep from * to * to end, turn.

Row 1: Ch 2 (count as hdc), hdc around first ch-1 sp, ch 1, *hdc around next ch-1 sp, ch 1*, rep from * to * to last 2 sts, sk next hdc, hdc in last st (top of tch), turn.

Rep row 1.

OPENWORK PATTERN

Multiple of 3 sts + 1 (also add 7 sts for base chain)

Foundation Row (RS): Dc in 8th ch from hook (count tch as hdc and ch-sp), *ch 1, sk 2 chs, dc in next ch*, rep from * to * to end, turn.

Row 1: Ch 5 (count as hdc and ch-sp), *dc in next dc, ch 2*, rep from * to * across, sk 2 chs in tch, dc in next ch, turn.

Rep row 1.

NOTE: *For the shell and stole instructions that follow, count the turning chain as a stitch. Unless the instructions indicate otherwise, work the last stitch of each row into the top of the turning chain of the previous row.*

Shell Back

String beads onto yarn (see "Beading" on page 30). With E/4 (3.5 mm) hook, ch 109 (119, 129, 139, 149).

Row 1: Hdc in 3rd ch from hook (count as hdc), *ch 1, sk 1 st, hdc in next ch*, rep from * to * to end, turn. [108 (118, 128, 138, 148) sts]

Row 2: As Offset Filet pat row 1.

Cont in pat until 12 (12, 12, 12½, 12½)" from beg.

ARMHOLE SHAPING

Next Row: *Sl st around ch-sp and in next hdc*, rep from * to * 1 (2, 3, 4, 5) more time(s), sl st around next ch-sp, ch 2 (count as hdc), *hdc around next ch-sp, ch 1*, rep from * to * to last 3, (4, 5, 6, 7) ch-sps, hdc around next ch-sp, turn. [98 (104, 110, 116, 122) sts]

Next Row: Ch 2 (count as hdc), sk first ch-sp, *hdc around next ch-sp, ch 1*, rep from * to * across to last hdc, sk last hdc, hdc in top of tch, turn. [96 (102, 108, 114, 120) sts]

BEADING

Next Row: As Offset Filet pat row 1, AT SAME TIME place 1 bead on every 2nd hdc, turn.

Next Row: As Offset Filet pat row 1.

Next Row: As Offset Filet pat row 1, AT SAME TIME place 1 bead on every alternate hdc to stagger placement.

Rep last 2 rows until 18 (18½, 19, 19½, 20)" from beg.

RIGHT SHOULDER SHAPING

Next Row: Work in pat across 28 (30, 32, 34, 36) sts, turn. Rem 68 (72, 76, 80, 84) sts unworked.

Next Row (Dec Row): Ch 2 (count as hdc), sk first ch-sp, hdc around next ch-sp, ch 1, *hdc around next ch-sp, ch 1*, rep from * to * to last 2 hdc, sk next hdc, hdc in last st, turn. [26 (28, 30, 32, 34) sts]

Work 1 row even in pat. Rep last dec row once. [24 (26, 28, 30, 32) sts]

Work even in pat until 20 (20½, 21, 21½, 22)" from beg. Fasten off.

LEFT SHOULDER SHAPING

Next Row: Working on last full row, sk 40 (42, 44, 46, 48) sts in center for back neck. Reattach yarn with sc around next ch-sp, ch 3, sk first hdc, *hdc around next ch-sp, ch 1*, rep from * to * to last ch-sp, hdc around last ch-sp, hdc in top of tch (no ch between 2 hdc made), turn. [28 (30, 32, 34, 36) sts]

Next Row (Dec Row): Ch 3 (count as hdc and ch-sp), hdc around first ch-sp, ch 1, *hdc around next ch-sp, ch 1*, rep from * to * across to last hdc and tch, sk next hdc, hdc in 2nd st from top of tch, turn. [26 (28, 30, 32, 34) sts]

Work 1 row even in pat. Rep last dec row once. [24 (26, 28, 30, 32) sts]

Work even in pat until same length as right shoulder. Fasten off.

Shell Front

Work as for shell back until 16 (16½, 17, 17½, 18)" from beg.

Shape shoulders as for shell back. Fasten off.

Finishing

With RS of front and back tog, sew shoulders and side seams.

HEM EDGING

With C/2 (3 mm) hook and RS facing you, attach yarn at one side seam.

Rnd 1: Sc in each st around lower edge, join start and end of edging with sl st. Fasten off.

NECK AND ARMHOLE EDGING

With C/2 (3 mm) hook and RS facing you, attach yarn at shoulder seam.

Rnd 1: Work evenly spaced sc around edge, join to first sc with sl st. Do not turn.

F O U N D A T I O N S

BEADING

Working beads into crocheted fabric requires a bit of planning, but is much easier than you might think. You thread the beads onto a ball of yarn first, and then, as you work, you pull a bead up whenever you want to place one in your garment. Unless the beads appear in the first few rows of stitching, you can start your work with a plain ball of yarn and switch to a bead-laden ball as you near the area where the beads are required.

To thread the beads onto the ball, first place the start of the yarn ball in the center of your beading wire, and fold the wire in half, trapping the strand in the fold. Next, hold the ends of the wire together and slide a bead onto them, all the way down the folded wire and onto the yarn. (If you run across any beads that won't slide down easily, don't waste time trying to use them; just set them aside.) Thread as many beads as you need.

When you're ready to place the first bead in your crocheted fabric, slide it up the yarn until it's at the crochet hook. Then work a stitch as usual. The bead will be trapped in the yarn wraps.

Rnd 2: Ch 1, rsc in first and each st, join to first st with sl st. Fasten off.

Stole

With H/8 (5 mm) hook, ch 11.

Row 1: Dc in 8th ch from hook (count tch as dc, ch-sp, dc), sk 2 chs, ch 2, dc in last ch, turn. [3 dc]

Row 2: Ch 7 (count as dc and ch-sp), dc in first dc (at base of tch just made), ch 2, dc in next dc, ch 2, sk 2 chs, (dc, ch 2, dc) in next ch of tch, turn. [5 dc]

Row 3: Place marker. Ch 7 (count as dc and ch-sp), dc in first dc (at base of tch just made), ch 2, *dc in next dc, ch 2*, rep from * to * to tch, ch 2, sk 2 chs (dc, ch 2, dc) in next ch of tch, turn. [7 dc]

Rep row 3 until 21 dc in row, turn.

Work even in Openwork pat row 1 until 36" from marker, turn. Remove marker.

Next Row: Ch 3 (count as dc), *dc in next dc, ch 2*, rep from * to * to tch, turn. Rem ch-1 sp and tch unworked. [20 dc]

Rep last row until 3 dc rem. Fasten off.

EDGING

Thread beads onto yarn. Attach yarn in any ch-sp along edge, *ch 1 around first ch-sp, ch 1 with 1 bead, ch 1, sc around next ch-sp*, rep from * to * around edge, join to first st with sl st. Fasten off.

Finishing

Block lightly on wrong side. Don't press.

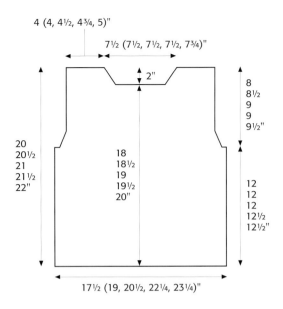

SHELL BACK

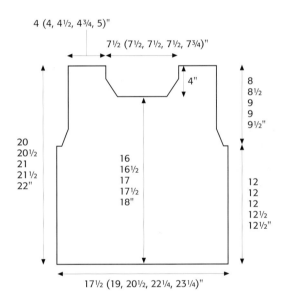

SHELL FRONT

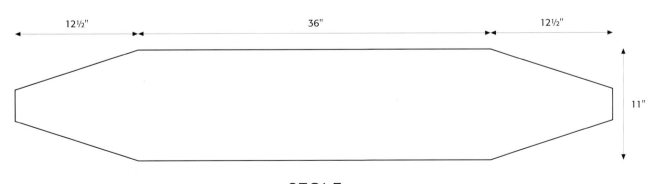

STOLE

Part of the Crew

BY JANE SNEDDEN PEEVER

*E*very wardrobe needs a casual, classic crew-neck sweater made with toasty, warm wool. (The yarn used in this sweater comes from an island off Canada's east coast.) If you're new to crocheting, you'll find that this project will add to your repertoire of skills by helping you learn how to double crochet around front and back posts.

DESIGN DETAILS

- Oversize
- Body length to high hip
- Drop shoulder, long sleeve
- Top of collar ribbing rests on collarbone

FEATURED STITCHES

Back post double crochet (BPDC); see page 110

Chain (ch); see page 99

Front post double crochet (FPDC); see page 110

Single crochet (sc); see page 100

Single crochet 2 together (sc2tog); see page 111

SIZING

To fit bust: 31½ (34¼, 37¼, 41, 43¼)"

Finished bust: 40 (44, 48, 52, 56)"

MATERIALS

8 (8, 9, 9, 10) skeins of Briggs & Little *Heritage* (100% wool: 4 ozs./113 g; 215 yds./196 m); #14 Sheep's Grey

Size 7 (4.5 mm) crochet hook

H/8 (5 mm) crochet hook

4 stitch markers

GAUGE

12 sts and 14 rows to 4" in Basketweave pattern, with H/8 (5 mm) hook

RIB PATTERN

NOTE: *Count the ch-3 turning chain as a double crochet. Don't work the next stitch of the new row into the base of the turning chain. Instead, work the new stitch into the top of the second stitch of the previous row. The process is the same when you're working the new stitch into the row below.*

Multiple of 2 sts + 1 (also add 3 sts for base chain)

Foundation Row: Dc in 4th ch from hook (count as 2 dc) and in each ch to end, turn.

Row 1: Ch 3 (count as dc), *BPDC in next st in row below, FPDC in next st in row below*, rep from * to * across to last st, BPDC in next st in row below, dc in last st, turn.

Row 2: Ch 3 (count as dc), *FPDC in next st in row below, BPDC in next st in row below*, rep from * to * across to last st, FPDC in last st in row below, dc in last st, turn.

Rep rows 1 and 2.

BASKETWEAVE PATTERN

NOTE: *Don't count the ch-1 turning chain at the start of the row as a stitch. In other words, start the new row with a single crochet in the first stitch of the previous row.*

Multiple of 12 sts + 1 (also add 1 st for base chain)

Foundation Row: Sc in 2nd ch from hook and in each ch to end, turn.

Rows 1, 3, 5, 7, 9, and 11 (WS): Ch 1, sc in first and each st to end, turn.

Rows 2, 4, and 6 (RS): Ch 1, sc in first st, *(FPDC in next st in row below, sc in next st) 3 times, sc in next 6 sts*, rep from * to * to end, turn.

Rows 8, 10, and 12: Ch 1, sc in first 7 sts, *(FPDC in next st in row below, sc in next st) 3 times, sc in next 6 sts*, rep from * to * to end, turn.

Repeat rows 1–12.

NOTE: *When the instructions call for increases and decreases in pattern rows, follow the instructions below.*

To Dec 1 St at Beg of Row: Ch 1, sc2tog, and work rem sts as directed.

To Inc at Beg and End of Rows 1, 3, 5, 7, 9, and 11: Ch 1, 2 sc in first st, sc in next and each st to last st, 2 sc in last st, turn.

Back

With size 7 (4.5 mm) hook, ch 63 (69, 75, 81, 87).

RIBBING

Row 1: Dc in 4th ch from hook (count as 2 dc) and in each ch to end, turn. [61 (67, 73, 79, 85) dc]

Work Rib pat, starting with row 1, until 2½" from beg.

BODY

Change to H/8 (5 mm) hook.

Row 1 (WS): Ch 1, sc in first and each st to end, turn.

X-Small, Medium, and X-Large Only

Row 2 (RS): Ch 1, sc in first st, *(FPDC in next st in previous row, sc in next st) 3 times, sc in next 6 sts*, rep from * to * to end, turn.

Next Row: As Basketweave pat row 3.

Next Row: As Basketweave pat row 4.

Small and Large Only

Row 2 (RS): Ch 1, sc in first 7 sts, *(FPDC in next st in previous row, sc in next st) 3 times, sc in each of next 6 sts*, rep from * to * to end, turn.

Next Row: As Basketweave pat row 3.

Next Row: As Basketweave pat row 10.

All Sizes

Cont in pat as established (small and large starting with row 11), until 25 (25, 26, 26, 27)" from beg. Fasten off.

Front

Work as for back until piece is 22 (22, 23, 23, 24)" from beg, ending with WS row completed.

LEFT SHOULDER SHAPING

Next Row (RS): Cont in pat as established across 26 (29, 31, 34, 36) sts, turn. Rem sts unworked.

Next Row: Ch 1, sc2tog (1 dec made), work in pat as established to end, turn. [25 (28, 30, 33, 35) sts]

Next Row: Ch 1, work in pat as established across to last st, turn. Don't work last st. [24 (27, 29, 32, 34) sts]

Cont in pat as established for 6 more rows, AT SAME TIME dec 1 st at neck edge every row. [18 (21, 23, 26, 28) sts]

Work even in pat as established until 25 (25, 26, 26, 27)" from beg. Fasten off.

RIGHT SHOULDER SHAPING

Next Row: With RS facing you, sk 8 (8, 10, 10, 12) sts in center (neckline), attach yarn with sl st in next st. Work across rem 26 (29, 31, 34, 36) sts in pat as established, turn.

Next Row (WS): Ch 1, work in pat as established across to last 2 sts, sc2tog (neck edge), turn. [25 (28, 30, 33, 35) sts]

Next Row: Ch 1, sc2tog, work in pat as established to end, turn. [24 (27, 29, 32, 34) sts]

Rep last 2 rows 3 more times. [18 (21, 23, 26, 28) sts]

Work even in pat as established until 25 (25, 26, 26, 27)" from beg. Fasten off.

Sleeve (Make 2)

With size 7 (4.5 mm) hook, ch 33.

RIBBING

Row 1: Dc in 4th ch from hook (count as 2 dc) and in each ch to end, turn. [31 sts]

Work in Rib pat, starting with row 1, until 2½" from beg.

ARM

Change to H/8 (5 mm) hook.

Row 1 (WS): Ch 1, sc in first and each st to end, turn.

Row 2: Ch 1, sc in first 7 sts, *(FPDC in next st in row below, sc in next st) 3 times, sc in next 6 sts*, rep from * to * to end, turn.

Row 3: As Basketweave pat row 9.

Cont in pat as established, AT SAME TIME inc 1 st at beg and end of every 2nd row 5 times, then every 4th row 10 times. [61 sts]

Work even in pat as established until 19½" from beg. Fasten off.

Neck Ribbing

With RS tog, join front and back at right shoulder.

Using size 7 (4.5 mm) hook and with RS facing you, attach yarn at left shoulder.

Row 1: Ch 3 (count as 1 dc), work 13 dc down left front of neck, 11 dc across center front of neck, 14 dc up right front of neck, and 27 dc across back of neck, ch 3 (count as 1 dc), turn. [66 dc]

Work in Rib pat, starting with row 1, until ribbing is 2½"
   deep. Fasten off.
With RS tog, sew front and back tog at left shoulder
   and ribbing.

Finishing

Spread joined, opened front and back flat on a table,
   with RS facing you. Place markers along each edge,
   10" from shoulder seams, to mark armholes. Position
   sleeve across joined pieces, RS down, with wider end
   between markers on one side and aligned with edge
   of armhole. Sew sleeve to body. Attach rem sleeve in
   same manner.
Remove markers. Refold body and sleeves, RS tog, aligning all matching edges. Join front to back by sewing
   up sides and along sleeve underarms.

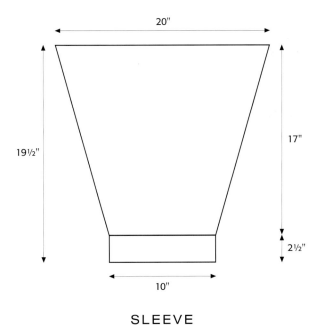

FRONT

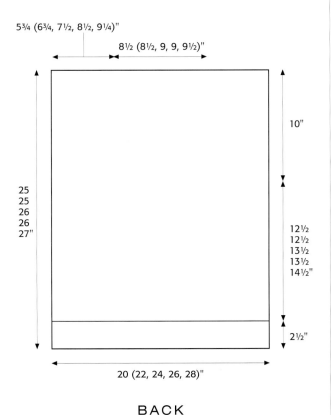

BACK

SLEEVE

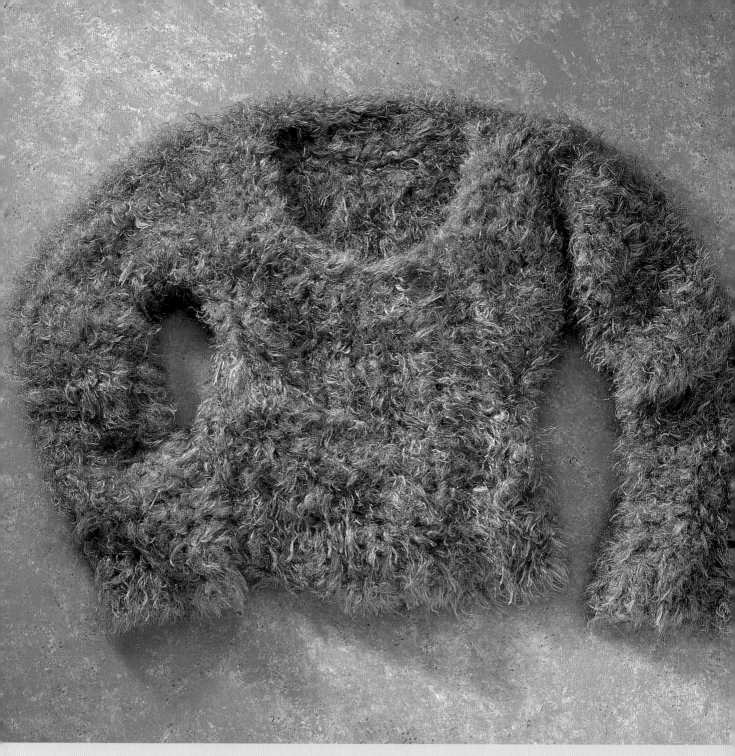

Cat's Meow

BY SUSAN HUXLEY

Feminine but not too sweet, the big-girl pink of this wonderful yarn zaps new life into a simple sweater. While fuzzy yarns can sometimes pose challenges to beginning crocheters, an easy stitch and a large hook make this project perfect for the eager-to-learn. In no time at all, you'll have an irresistibly soft sweater. Wear it with jeans for a glamorous daytime look, or show it off with a full-length taffeta skirt the next time you go to a formal party.

DESIGN DETAILS

- Fitted
- Body length to below waist
- Full-length sleeve worked as part of body
- Scoop neck

FEATURED STITCHES

Chain (ch); see page 99

Chain-space (ch-sp); see page 111

Half double crochet (hdc); see page 103

Slip stitch (sl st); see page 102

SIZING

To fit bust: 31½ (37¼, 37¼, 41, 41)"

Finished bust: 35 (40½, 40½, 45½, 45½)"

MATERIALS

7 (8, 8, 9, 9) balls of Adriafil *Stars A & S* (50% viscose, 50% nylon: 1¾ ozs./50 g; 71 yds./65 m); #83 Pink

N/15 (10 mm) crochet hook

4 stitch markers

7 yds. smooth, lightweight pink yarn (for seaming)

GAUGE

NOTE: *To count pattern repeats in a row, hold the swatch up to a light source and count every V-shaped "hole." Each one is the center of a pattern repeat. It may seem as if you're counting every second hole because there's also an inverted, V-shaped hole between each pattern repeat.*

3 pat reps (in a row) to 4¼" and 7 rows to 4½" in Half Double Crochet V pattern

HALF DOUBLE CROCHET V PATTERN

Multiple of 3 sts (add 3 sts for base chain)

Foundation Row: (Hdc, ch 1, hdc) in 4th ch from hook, *sk 2 chs, (hdc, ch 1, hdc) in next ch*, rep from * to * to last 2 chs, sk 1 ch, hdc in last ch, turn.

Row 1: Ch 2 (count as hdc), *sk next hdc, (hdc, ch 1, hdc) in next ch-sp* (1 pat rep made), rep from * to * to last hdc and tch, sk 1 hdc, hdc around tch, turn.

Rep row 1.

Back

Ch 33 (39, 39, 45, 45).

Row 1: As pat foundation row, turn. [10 (12, 12, 14, 14) pat reps]

Row 2: As pat row 1, turn.

Work even in pat for 6".

Next Row: Ch 3 (count as hdc and ch-sp), hdc in first st (base of tch), *sk 1 hdc, (hdc, ch 1, hdc) around next ch-sp*, rep from * to * to last hdc and tch, sk 1 hdc, (hdc, ch 1, hdc) around tch, turn. [12 (14, 14, 16, 16) pat reps]

Next Row: Ch 2 (count as hdc), (hdc, ch 1, hdc) around first ch-sp, *sk 1 ch, (hdc, ch 1, hdc) around next ch-sp*, rep from * to * to last hdc and tch, sk 1 hdc, (hdc, ch 1, hdc) around tch, hdc around tch 1 more time, turn. [12 (14, 14, 16, 16) pat reps and 2 edge sts]

Next Row: As pat row 1, turn.

Work even in pat until 10¼ (10½, 11, 10¾, 11)" from beg. Don't turn.

UPPER SLEEVES SET-UP

NOTE: *Make sure the body isn't twisted as you start working into it. You want to work into the top of the chain stitches and the top of the uppermost row of the body stitches.*

Left Sleeve: Place marker, ch 23. Fasten off.

Right Sleeve: Join yarn with sl st around tch at start of row just worked (top row of opposite side of body), place marker, ch 24. Turn.

UPPER SLEEVES

Row 1; Right Sleeve: As pat foundation row to 2 chs before marker, sk 2 chs, sk 1 hdc, (hdc, ch 1, hdc) between next 2 hdc (edge st and start of first pat rep in body); then continue with body.

Body: Sk 1 hdc, (hdc, ch 1, hdc) around next ch-sp, work in pat to marker, (hdc, ch 1, hdc) between last 2 hdc (last pat rep and edge st); then continue with left sleeve.

Left Sleeve: *Sk next hdc, sk 2 chs, (hdc, ch 1, hdc) in next ch*, rep from * to * to last 2 chs, sk 1 ch, hdc in last ch. Don't turn. [28 (30, 30, 32, 32) pat reps]

Large and X-Large Only

Next Row: Turn, work as for pat row 1. Don't turn.

LOWER SLEEVES SET-UP

NOTE: *Instructions for the lower sleeves are set up for sizes X-small, small, and medium. For sizes large and X-large, follow the same instructions, but work the right sleeve first.*

Left Sleeve: Place marker, ch 20 (23, 23, 26, 26). Fasten off.

Right Sleeve: Join yarn with sl st around tch at start of row just worked, place marker, ch 21 (24, 24, 27, 27). Don't turn.

LOWER SLEEVES

Row 1: As upper sleeves row 1 for right sleeve, body, and left sleeve, turn. [42 (46, 46, 50, 50) pat reps]

Row 2: As pat row 1 to end of opposite sleeve, turn. Remove markers. Work even in pat for 6 rows. Fasten off.

Front

Work as for back to lower sleeves set-up. (Upper sleeves completed.)

FIRST LOWER SLEEVE AND SHOULDER SHAPING

NOTE: *This is the left side of the body for sizes X-small, small, and medium; and the right side for sizes large and X-large.* NOTE ALSO: *When instructions say "place marker," move up the closest marker in the previous row (if there is one).*

Place marker, ch 21 (24, 24, 27, 27), turn.

Next Row (Dec Row 1): As pat foundation row until 20 (22, 22, 24, 24) pat reps worked, hdc around next ch-sp, turn. Rem 14 (15, 15, 16, 16) pat reps unworked.

Next Row (Dec Row 2): Ch 2 (count as hdc), sk next pat rep, (hdc, ch 1, hdc) around next pat rep, place marker, work in pat to end, turn. [19 (21, 21, 23, 23) pat reps]

Next Row (Dec Row 3): As pat row 1 to marker, hdc around last ch-1 sp, place marker, turn. [18 (20, 20, 22, 22) pat reps]

Work even in pat for 5 rows, placing marker at neck edge of each row.

SECOND SHOULDER SHAPING

Attach yarn to rem upper sleeve with sl st around tch at beg of row.

Work as for first lower sleeve and shoulder shaping. Fasten off.

Finishing

Fold back in half, matching the edges of sides and sleeves. Place marker at neckline fold to mark center back. Unfold back. Place marker 4¼" from one side of center back marker to mark one edge of neckline. Place another marker the same distance away, but on opposite side. Remove center stitch marker.

With RS tog and using smooth, lightweight yarn, sew front to back at sides, sleeve underarms, tops of sleeves, and shoulders. Remove all markers, and turn sweater RS out.

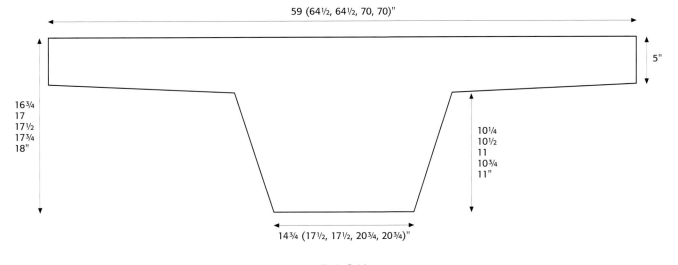

59 (64½, 64½, 70, 70)"

5"

16¾
17
17½
17¾
18"

10¼
10½
11
10¾
11"

14¾ (17½, 17½, 20¾, 20¾)"

BACK

8½"

25¼ (28, 28, 30¾, 30¾)"

5¼"

5"

16¾
17
17½
17¾
18"

10¼
10½
11
10¾
11"

14¾ (17½, 17½, 20¾, 20¾)"

FRONT

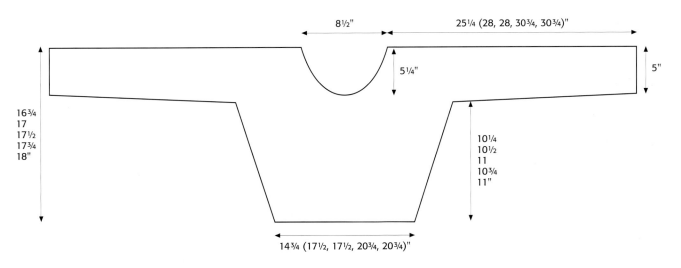

Granny's Attic

BY NANCY BROWN

*Y*ou'll give designer Nancy Brown a rave review of this vest, especially when you discover that she's created it with simple granny squares. The easy-to-make half squares and triangles replace traditional armhole and neckline shaping. To link the squares visually, Nancy worked each one with doubled yarn strands. Combining strands of different colors in this manner provides endless possibilities for harmonious combinations.

DESIGN DETAILS

• Semifitted
• Body length to below waist
• Yarn doubled for all stitching

FEATURED STITCHES

NOTE: *For extra guidance, see "Crocheting with Doubled Yarn" on page 42.*

Chain (ch); see page 99
Chain-space (ch-sp); see page 111
Double crochet (dc); see page 103
Single crochet (sc); see page 100
Slip stitch (sl st); see page 102

SIZING

To fit bust: 31½ (34¼, 37¼, 41, 43¼)"
Finished bust: 36 (39, 42, 45, 48)"

MATERIALS

NOTE: *The size of the hook you use to make the granny squares will determine the size of the vest.*

Skacel *Fortissima* (75% virgin wool, 25% nylon: 1¾ ozs./50 g; 229 yds./210 m): 3 (3, 4, 4, 5) balls of #88 Brown Tweed; and 4 (4, 5, 5, 6) balls of #02 Black
Crochet hook (for granny squares): X-small–G/6 (4.25 mm); Small–H/8 (5 mm); Medium–I/9 (5.5 mm); Large–J/10 (6 mm); X-large–K/10.5 (7 mm)
Crochet hook (for bands) one size smaller than above
8 stitch markers
Five ⅝" buttons

GAUGE

1 square is 3 (3¼, 3½, 3¾, 4)". Use hook G (H, I, J, K) to make all squares, half squares, and triangles.

NOTE: *In the instructions and the color chart on page 44, A = 2 strands Brown Tweed, B = 1 strand Brown Tweed and 1 strand Black, C = 2 strands Black.*

Square 1

With A, ch 5, join start and end of ch with sl st to form a ring.

Rnd 1 (RS): Ch 3 (count as dc), 2 dc in ring, ch 3, *3 dc in ring, ch 3*, rep from * to * 2 more times, join with sl st in top of beg ch-3, turn. Place marker on RS of work. [4 ch-3 sps for corners]

Rnd 2: Ch 1, sl st in next ch-3 sp, ch 3 (count as dc), (2 dc, ch 3, 3 dc, ch 1) in same ch-3 sp, *(3 dc, ch 3, 3 dc, ch 1) in next ch-3 sp*, rep from * to * 2 more times, join with sl st in top of beg ch-3, turn. [4 ch-3 sps for corners]

Rnd 3: Ch 1, sl st in next ch-1 sp, ch 3 (count as dc), 2 dc in same ch-1 sp, ch 1, (3 dc, ch 3, 3 dc, ch 1) in next ch-3 sp, *(3 dc, ch 1) in next ch-1 sp, (3 dc, ch 3, 3 dc, ch 1) in next ch-3 sp*, rep from * to * 2 more times, join with sl st in top of beg ch-3. Fasten off. [4 ch-3 sps for corners with a 3-dc box between each corner]

Square 2

With B, ch 5, join start and end of ch with sl st to form a ring.

Rnds 1 and 2: Work as for square 1.

Rnd 3 (Joining Rnd): Ch 1, sl st in next ch-1 sp, ch 3 (count as dc), 2 dc in same sp, ch 1, (3 dc, ch 1) in next ch-3 sp, with WS of square 1 and square 2 tog, sc in any ch-3 corner of square 1, ch 1, 3 dc in same ch-3 sp of square 2, sc in next ch-1 sp of square 1, 3 dc in next ch-1 sp of square 2, sc in next ch-1 sp of square 1, 3 dc in next corner ch-3 sp of square 2, ch 1, sc in next corner sp of square 1, ch 1, 3 dc in same corner ch-3 sp of square 2, ch 1. Complete rnd 3 by working (3 dc, ch 1) in each ch-1 sp and (3 dc, ch 3, 3 dc, ch 1) in each ch-3 sp, sl st in beg ch-3 to join rnd. Fasten off.

Squares 3–13

Following color chart on page 44, work and attach
squares as for square 2. Join edges in the sequence
shown in the chart, making sure to attach square 13
to top of square 1.

Square 14

With A, ch 5, join start and end of ch with sl st to form
a ring.

Rnds 1 and 2: Work as for square 1.

Rnd 3 (Joining Rnd): Ch 1, sl st in next ch-1 sp, ch 3,
2 dc in same sp, ch 1, (3 dc, ch 1) in next ch-3 sp, with
WS of squares 13 and 14 tog, sc in ch-3 corner of
square 13, ch 1, 3 dc in same ch-3 sp of square 14, sc
in next ch-1 sp of square 13, 3 dc in next ch-1 sp of
square 14, sc in next ch-1 sp of square 13, 3 dc in next
corner ch-3 sp of square 14, ch 1, sc in corner ch-3 sp
of square 1, ch 1, 3 dc in same corner ch-3 sp of
square 14, join next side of square 14 to square 2 as
before. Complete rnd 3 as explained for square 2.

Squares 15–26

Following color chart on page 44, work and attach
squares as for square 14.

Triangle 27

With A, ch 5, join start and end of ch with sl st to form
a ring.

Row 1 (RS): Ch 3 (count as dc), 2 dc in ring, ch 3, *3 dc
in ring, ch 3*, rep from * to * 1 more time, 3 dc in
ring, turn. [3 ch-3 sps for corners]

Row 2: Ch 1, sl st in each of next 3 dc, sl st in next
ch-3 sp, ch 3 (count as dc), 2 dc in same sp, ch 3,
3 dc in same sp, ch 1, *(3 dc, ch 3, 3 dc, ch 1) in
next ch-3 sp*, rep from * to * 1 more time, turn.
[3 ch-3 sps for corners]

Row 3 (Joining Row): Ch 1, sl st in each of next 3 dc,
sl st in next ch-3 sp, [ch 3 (count as dc), 2 dc, ch 1]
in next ch-3 sp, and join to squares 26 and 15 in the
established manner.

Rem Squares and Triangles

Following color chart on page 44, work and attach
triangles and squares.

X-Small and Small Only

Following color chart on page 44 and the instructions
for half squares 55–60, work and attach remaining
half squares.

HALF SQUARE 55

With C, ch 5, join start and end of ch with sl st to form
a ring.

Row 1 (RS): Ch 3, 2 dc in ring, ch 3 (count as dc), 3 dc in
ring, ch 3, 3 dc in ring, turn. [2 ch-3 sps for corners]

Row 2: Ch 4 (count as dc and ch-1 sp), *(3 dc, ch 3, 3 dc)
in next ch-3 sp, ch 1*, rep from * to * 1 more time, dc

F O U N D A T I O N S
CROCHETING WITH DOUBLED YARN

Working with doubled strands of yarn makes it possible to combine yarns of different weights and thickness in a garment, and to maintain a consistent gauge and fabric thickness throughout. For special effects, try combining two different colors, or a fuzzy or sparkly yarn with a smooth strand.

Start by winding the two balls or skeins together to make one. If your local yarn shop has a winder that feeds the strands from the inside of each ball or skein, consider having the job done there.

To work with the doubled yarn, just treat the two strands as if they were one. Make a slip knot on your hook as usual, and then, whenever the stitch or instructions call for a YO, wrap both strands around the hook.

in 3rd ch of tch, turn. [2 ch-2 sps for corners and 2 ch-1 sps]

Row 3 (Joining Row): Ch 4 (count as dc and ch-1 sp), 3 dc in next ch-1 sp, ch 1, 3 dc in next ch-3 sp, ch 1, with WS tog, sc in ch-3 sp of square 45, ch 1, 3 dc in same sp of square 55, sc in next ch-1 sp of square 45, 3 dc in next ch-1 sp of square 55, sc in next ch-1 sp of square 45, 3 dc in next ch-3 sp of square 55, ch 1, sc in next ch-3 sp of square 45, ch 1, 3 dc in same sp of square 55, ch 1, 3 dc around tch, ch 1, dc in 3rd st from end of tch. Fasten off.

HALF SQUARES 56 AND 60

With C, work and attach as for half square 55.

HALF SQUARE 57

With A, ch 5, join start and end of ch with sl st to form a ring.

Rows 1 and 2: Work as for half square 55.

Row 3 (Joining Row): Ch 3, sc in first ch-1 sp of square 56, 3 dc in next ch-1 sp of square 57, sc in next ch-1 sp of 56, 3 dc in next ch-3 sp of square 57, ch 1, sc in ch-3 sp of square 46, ch 1, 3 dc in same ch-3 sp of square 57, cont along next edge of square 57 while joining it to top of square 47.

HALF SQUARES 58 AND 59

Following color chart on page 44, work and attach as for half square 57.

Finishing

Fold ends so that RS of each front rests on back; then sew shoulders together.

BUTTON BAND

Row 1: With RS of left front facing you, and using smaller hook, join C at beg of row 3 of square 37. Work evenly spaced sc to end of row 3 of triangle 51, only working sc in the ends (3 dc) of the last row of each triangle, turn.

Row 2: Ch 1, sc in each sc to end.

Large and X-Large Only

Work 2 more rows sc.

All Sizes

Fasten off. Place stitch markers for button placement.

BUTTONHOLE BAND

Row 1: With RS of right front facing you, and using smaller hook, join C at beg of row 3 of triangle 54. Work evenly spaced sc to end of row 3 of triangle 44, turn.

Medium, Large, and X-Large Only

Next Row: Sc in each sc to end, turn.

All Sizes

Next Row: Ch 1, sc in each sc to end, working (ch 1, sk 1 st) for every buttonhole, using markers on left front as guides, CONT working 1 sc evenly spaced around entire vest, working sc in each point of triangle with ch-3 between. Fasten off.

NECK EDGING

With RS facing you, attach yarn in first sc at top of buttonhole band on right front. *Sk 1 st, (sc, dc, sc) in next st, sk 1 st, sc in next st*, rep from * to * to top of button band on left front. Fasten off.

BOTTOM EDGING

Row 1: With RS facing you, attach yarn in first sc at bottom of button band on left front, *sk 1 st, (sc, dc, sc) in next st, sk 1 st, sc in next st*, rep from * to * to bottom of buttonhole band on right front. Fasten off.

ARMHOLE EDGING

Rnd 1: With RS facing you, attach yarn between triangles 27 and 28 for the left underarm and triangles 33 and 34 for the right underarm. Work 1 rnd of sc evenly spaced around armhole, working 1 sc in each point of triangle and ch-3 between the points, ending with sl st in beg sc, turn.

Rnd 2: Ch 1, *sk 1 st, (sc, dc, sc) in next st, sk 1 st, sc in next st*, rep from * to * around armhole. Fasten off. Sew in all ends, and sew on buttons. Remove markers.

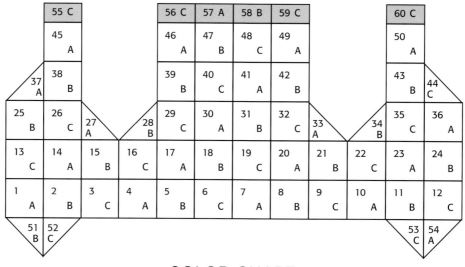

COLOR CHART

Shaded areas apply to sizes X-small and small only

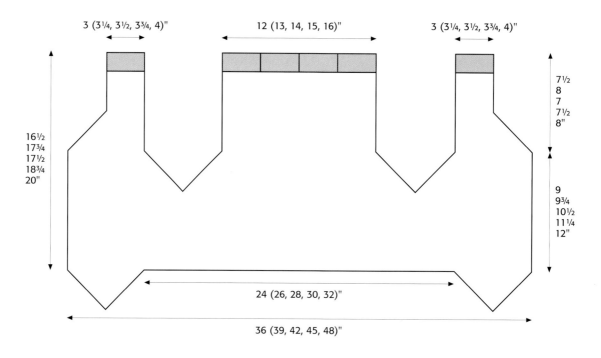

VEST

Homespun Hug

BY TRICIA CRICHTON

*T*his comfortable cardigan is roomy enough to layer over another sweater on very cold days, but cool enough to wear over a lightweight shirt on warmer ones. Gentle shaping by using stitch variations rather than increases and decreases eliminates bulk at the bust and waist.

DESIGN DETAILS

- Very loose fitting
- Body length to upper thigh
- Set-in sleeve with moderate cap shaping
- Wrap front

FEATURED STITCHES

Chain (ch); see page 99

Double crochet (dc); see page 103

Double crochet 2 together (dc2tog); see page 112

Half double crochet (hdc); see page 103

Half double crochet 2 tog (hdc2tog); see page 112

Single crochet (sc); see page 100

Slip stitch (sl st); see page 102

SIZING

To fit bust: 31½ (34¼, 37¼, 41, 43¼)"

Finished bust: 41 (42, 45, 45, 51)"

MATERIALS

7 skeins Lion Brand *Homespun* (98% acrylic, 2% polyester: 6 ozs./170 g; 185 yds./168 m) #336 Barrington

J/10 (6 mm) crochet hook

14 stitch markers

GAUGE

20 sts to 7¼" and 10 rows to 6½" in dc

NOTE: *Some rows start with 1 chain stitch. This ch-1 turning chain doesn't count as a stitch, so work the first stitch of the row into the base of the turning chain. Other rows start with 3 chain stitches. This ch-3 turning chain does count as a stitch, so work the first stitch of the new row into the next stitch of the previous row; only work into the first stitch (the base of the turning chain) when told to make an increase.* NOTE ALSO: *Before you begin, take a look at the assembly guide on page 49.*

The arrows in this diagram indicate the direction in which each garment piece is worked.

Back (Make 2)

NOTE: *Continue using same marker throughout back, moving it up to current row whenever asked to "place marker."*

Ch 71 (73, 74, 76, 81).

Row 1 (Center Back): Sc in 2nd ch from hook, sc in next 51 (53, 53, 54, 57) sts, place marker, sc in each ch to end (neck edge), turn. [70 (72, 73, 75, 80) sts]

Row 2: Ch 2 (count as hdc), hdc in next and each st to marker, dc in each of next 15 (15, 15, 20, 17) sts, hdc in each of next 31 (32, 32, 16, 24) sts, dc in each st to end, turn.

Row 3: Ch 3 (count as dc), dc in next 15 (17, 17, 54, 20) sts, hdc in each of next 13 (13, 13, 0, 12) sts, dc in each of next 22 (23, 23, 0, 25) sts, place marker, dc in each of next 7 (7, 7, 8, 9) sts, hdc in each st to end, turn.

Rep last 2 rows 2 (2, 2, 3, 3) more times.

Rep row 2 one more time.

X-Small, Small, and Medium Only

Row 9: Ch 3 (count as dc), dc in next 15 (17, 17) sts, hdc in each of next 13 (13, 13) sts, dc in each of next 22 (23, 23) sts, place marker, dc in each of next 7 (7, 7) sts, hdc in each st across to last 2 sts, hdc2tog, turn. [69 (71, 72) sts]

Row 10: As row 2, turn.

All Sizes

Row 11: Ch 3 (count as dc), dc in next 15 (17, 17, 54, 20) sts, hdc in each of next 13 (13, 13, 0, 12) sts, dc in each of next 22 (23, 23, 0, 25) sts, place marker, dc in each of next 7 (7, 7, 8, 9) sts, hdc in each st across to last 2 sts, hdc2tog, turn. [68 (70, 71, 74, 79) sts]

Row 12: Ch 2 (count as hdc), hdc2tog, hdc in next and each st to marker, dc in each of next 15 (15, 15, 20, 17) sts, hdc in each of next 31 (32, 32, 16, 24) sts, dc in each st to end, turn. [67 (69, 70, 73, 78) sts]

Row 13: As row 11. [66 (68, 69, 72, 77) sts]

X-Small, Small, Medium, and X-Large Only

Row 14: As row 2.

Large Only

Row 14: As row 12, turn. [71 sts]

All Sizes

Row 15: As row 11, turn. [65 (67, 68, 70, 76) sts]

X-Large Only

Row 16: As row 2, turn.

Row 17: As row 11, turn. [75 sts]

All Sizes

Next Row: Ch 1, sc in first and each st to end. Fasten off.

Front (Make 2)

Ch 66 (68, 69, 71, 76).

Row 1 (Side of Garment): Sc in 2nd ch and in each ch to end, turn. [65 (67, 68, 70, 75) sts]

Row 2: Ch 3 (count as dc), dc in next 15 (16, 21, 18, 19) sts, place marker, hdc in each of next 17 (17, 17, 16, 17) sts, place marker, dc in each of next 16 (16, 13, 17, 18) sts, place marker, hdc in each of next 4 (4, 4, 5, 5) sts, place marker, hdc in each of next 4 (4, 4, 5, 5) sts, place marker, sc in each of next 4 (4, 4, 4, 5) sts, place marker, sc in each st to end, turn.

NOTE: *On every row for the rest of the front, as you encounter markers, move them from the previous row to the same position in the current row.*

Row 3: Ch 1, 2 sc in first st (shoulder inc made), sc in next and each st to marker, hdc in each st to next marker, hdc in each st to next marker, dc in each st to end, turn. [66 (68, 69, 71, 76) sts]

Rep last 2 rows 3 more times.

Rep row 2 one more time. [69 (71, 72, 74, 79) sts]

X-Small and Small Only

Row 11: Ch 1, sc in first and each st to first marker, hdc in each st to next marker, hdc in each st to next marker, dc in each st to end, turn.

Medium, Large, and X-Large Only

Row 11: As row 3. [(73, 75, 80) sts]

Rep rows 2 and 3 once. [(74, 76, 81) sts]

All Sizes

Next Row: Ch 3 (count as dc), dc in next and each st to first marker, hdc in each st to next marker, dc in each st to next marker, hdc in each st to next marker, hdc in each st to next marker, sc in each st to next marker, turn. Rem 9 (10, 11, 11, 12) sts unworked. [60 (61, 63, 65, 69) sts]

Next Row: Sl st to first marker, hdc in next and each st to next marker, dc in each st to end, turn. [56 (57, 59, 61, 64) sts]

Next Row: Ch 3 (count as dc), dc in each st to first marker, hdc in each st to next marker, dc in each st to next marker, hdc in each st to next marker, turn. Rem 4 (4, 4, 5, 5) sts unworked. [52 (53, 55, 56, 59) sts]

Next Row: Sl st to first marker, sl st in next st, ch 3 (count as dc), dc in next and each st to end, turn. [48 (49, 51, 51, 54) sts]

X-Large Only

Next Row: Ch 3 (count as dc), dc in next and each st to first marker, hdc in each st to next marker, dc in next and each st to end, turn.

Next Row: Ch 3 (count as dc), dc in next and each st to end.

All Sizes

Fasten off.

Sleeve (Make 4)

Ch 63 (64, 63, 67, 66).

Row 1 (Underarm): Dc in 4th ch from hook (count as 2 dc), dc in each of next 18 (18, 17, 21, 22) chs, place marker, hdc in each of next 28 chs, sc in each ch to end, turn. [61 (62, 61, 65, 64) sts]

NOTE: *On every row for the rest of the sleeve, as you encounter markers, move them from the previous row to the same position in the current row.*

Row 2: Ch 1, sc in first 28 sc, hdc in each hdc to marker, dc in next and each st to end, turn.

Row 3: Ch 3 (count as dc), 2 dc in next st twice, dc in each dc to marker, hdc in each of next 28 sts, sc in next and each st to end, turn. [63 (64, 63, 67, 66) sts]

Rep last 2 rows 1 more time. [65 (66, 65, 69, 68) sts]

Rep row 2 one more time.

Row 7: Ch 3 (count as dc), 2 dc in next st 2 (2, 2, 2, 1) time(s), dc in each dc to marker, hdc in each of next 28 sts, sc in next and each st to end, turn. [67 (68, 67, 71, 69) sts]

Row 8: As row 2, turn.

Row 9: Ch 3 (count as dc), 2 dc in next st 2 (2, 2, 1, 2) time(s), dc in each dc to marker, hdc in each of next 28 sts, sc in next and each st to end, turn. [69 (70, 69, 72, 71) sts]

Row 10: Ch 1, sc in first 28 sts, hdc in next and each hdc to marker, hdc in next 14 sts, dc in next and each st to last st, 2 dc in last st. Fasten off. [70 (71) sts]

Medium, Large, and X-Large Only

Row 10: As row 2, turn.

Row 11: As row 3, turn. [(71, 74, 73) sts]

Medium and Large Only

Fasten off.

X-Large Only

Rep rows 2 and 3 once. Fasten off. [75 sts]

Collar

Ch 162 (168, 171, 181, 193).

Row 1: Sc in 2nd ch from hook and each ch to end. [161 (167, 170, 180, 192) sts]

Place markers in foll sts:

X-small: 12, 21, 46, 50, 52, 66, 74, 88, 96, 110, 112, 116, 141, 150.

Small: 12, 22, 48, 52, 54, 68, 77, 91, 100, 114, 116, 120, 146, 156.

Medium: 12, 22, 33, 52, 54, 72, 79, 92, 99, 117, 119, 138, 149, 159.

Large: 12, 23, 35, 46, 57, 65, 80, 101, 116, 124, 135, 146, 158, 169.

X-large: 13, 25, 37, 54, 56, 64, 80, 113, 129, 137, 139, 156, 168, 180.

Fasten off.

Join yarn in 7th marker from beg.

Row 2: Working toward center, sl st in next 2 sts, sc in next 2 sts, hdc in next 2 sts, dc in each ch until 7 sts from next marker, hdc in each of next 2 sts, sc in each of next 2 sts, sl st in each of next 2 sts. Fasten off.

Rep last row 6 more times, joining yarn for each row 1 marker closer to beg of row 1 ch and always working in same direction.

Row 8: Join yarn in first st of base ch and work across as row 2. Fasten off.

Finishing

With RS tog and edges matching, sew left back to right back at center back. Sew front pieces at the shoulder. Also join front and back pieces at the sides for 16¼ (17, 17, 17, 17¾)" from the hem.

With RS tog and edges matching, sew 2 sleeve pieces tog along the long vertical edge. Fold sleeve in half vertically, RS tog. Join underarm edges with a line of sl sts. Rep to assemble rem sleeve pieces.

Turn sleeve RS out. Then slide sleeve into body until it's at an armhole. Align underarm and side seams, and match edge of sleeve with edge of armhole. Slip stitch the edges tog. (For a better fit, the sleeves are designed to be a slightly different size than the armholes of the sweater body, so ease the edges tog as you join them.) Rep to make, insert, and join rem sleeve to body. Remove markers.

Spread sweater out on a large, flat surface, with RS of front facing up. Align one end of collar, WS down, along one front edge of sweater. Butt collar and front edge tog. Using a running stitch, sew this portion of the collar in place, up to beg of neckline curve. Fasten off. Rep to sew other side of collar to corresponding edge of front. Sew rem portion of collar to body, adjusting collar by distributing its length around neckline if necessary. Both sides of collar will be visible on the finished garment, so sew carefully.

EDGING

Join yarn to cuff with sc at underarm seam. Work reverse sc in end of each row around cuff, join end of rnd to beg with sl st. Fasten off. Rep with other cuff.

Join yarn to hem with sc at side seam. Work reverse sc in end of each row; st around hem, front, and collar edge; and return to first sc. Join end of rnd to beg with sl st. Fasten off.

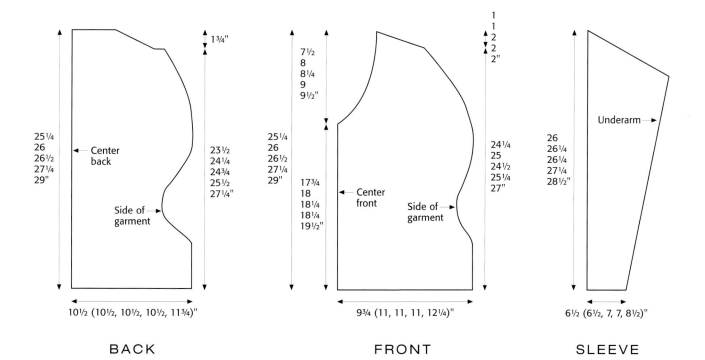

BACK

25¼
26
26½
27¼
29"

Center back

Side of garment

1¾"

23½
24¼
24¾
25½
27¼"

10½ (10½, 10½, 10½, 11¾)"

FRONT

7½
8
8¼
9
9½"

25¼
26
26½
27¼
29"

17¾
18
18¼
18¼
19½"

Center front

Side of garment

1
1
2
2
2"

24¼
25
24½
25¼
27"

9¾ (11, 11, 11, 12¼)"

SLEEVE

26
26¼
26¼
27¼
28½"

Underarm

6½ (6½, 7, 7, 8½)"

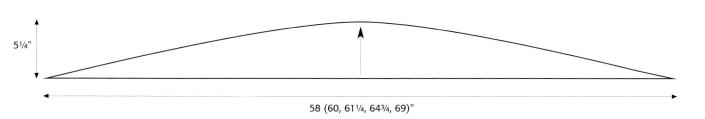

5¼"

58 (60, 61¼, 64¾, 69)"

COLLAR

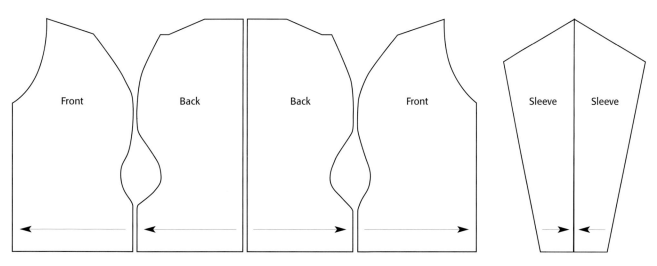

Front   Back   Back   Front   Sleeve   Sleeve

ASSEMBLY GUIDE

Double Take

BY JANE SNEDDEN PEEVER

*B*et *you're thinking, "This can't be a knit—it's in a crochet book!" Well, you're right. The designer created the popular, bulky "knitted" rib effect by working in the back loop of each stitch on alternate rows as she crocheted the sweater from side to side.*

DESIGN DETAILS

- Loose fitting
- Body length to high hip
- Drop shoulder, long sleeve
- Cowl collar widens slightly from base

FEATURED STITCHES

Back post double crochet (BPDC); see page 110

Chain (ch); see page 99

Double crochet (dc); page 103

Front post double crochet (FPDC); see page 110

Half double crochet (hdc); see page 103

Single crochet (sc); see page 100

Single crochet 2 together (sc2tog); see page 111

Single crochet in back loop only (sc in blo); see page 109

SIZING

To fit bust: 31½ (34¼, 37¼, 41, 43¼)"

Finished bust: 38 (42, 46, 50, 54)"

MATERIALS

9 (9, 10, 10, 11) skeins of Reynolds *Lopi* (100% wool:
  3½ ozs./100 g; 109 yds./100 m); #0054 Ash Heather

J/10 (6 mm) crochet hook

K/10.5 (7 mm) crochet hook

8 stitch markers

GAUGE

10 sts and 8 rows to 4" in Rib pattern, with
  K/10.5 (7 mm) hook

RIB PATTERN

NOTE: *On row 1, count the ch-2 turning chain that starts
each row as a stitch. After making the turning chain,
don't make a stitch into the stitch that the turning chain
is built on. Instead, work into the next stitch. Remember
to work the last double crochet of each row into the top
of the turning chain in the previous row. On row 2,
don't count the ch-1 turning chain at the start of the row
as a stitch. In other words, work the first single crochet
into the first stitch of the previous row.*

Worked over any number of sts (add 1 st for base chain)

Foundation Row (RS): Sc in 2nd ch from hook and in
  each ch to end, turn.

Row 1 (WS): Ch 2 (count as hdc), hdc in next and each
  sc to end, turn.

Row 2: Ch 1, sc in blo of first and each st to end, turn.

Rep rows 1 and 2.

Back

With K/10.5 (7 mm) hook, ch 46 (46, 47, 48, 48).

Row 1: Sc in 2nd ch from hook and in each ch across to
  end, turn. Place marker on RS of work (not at edge).
  [45 (45, 46, 47, 47) sts]

Row 2: As Rib pat row 1. [45 (45, 46, 47, 47) sts]

Work even in pat as established, until 19 (21, 23, 25, 27)"
  from beg. Fasten off.

Front

Work as for back until 5 (6, 7, 8, 9)" from beg, ending
  with pat row 1 completed.

NECKLINE SHAPING

Next Row (RS): Cont in pat to last 5 sts, sc2tog, turn.
  Rem 3 sts unworked. [41 (41, 42, 43, 43) sts]

Next Row: Ch 1, sc2tog, hdc in next and each sc to end,
  turn. [40 (40, 41, 42, 42) sts]

Next Row: Ch 1, sc in first and each st to last 2 sts,
  sc2tog, turn. [39 (39, 40, 41, 41) sts]

Rep last 2 rows 1 more time.

Work even in pat as established on rem 37 (37, 38, 39,
  39) sts until 14 (15, 16, 17, 18)" from beg, ending with
  pat row 1 completed.

Next Row: Ch 1, sc in first and each st across to last st,
  2 sc in last st, turn. [38 (38, 39, 40, 40) sts]

Next Row: Ch 2 (count as hdc), 2 sc in next sc, hdc in
  next and each st to end, turn. [39 (39, 40, 41, 41) sts]

Rep last 2 rows 1 more time.

Next Row: Ch 1, sc in first and each st across to last st, 2 sc in last st, turn. [42 (42, 43, 44, 44) sts]

Next Row: Ch 4, hdc in 3rd ch from hook (count as 2 hdc), hdc in next and each st to end, turn.

Work even in pat as established until 19 (21, 23, 25, 27)" from beg. Fasten off.

Sleeve (Make 2)

With K/10.5 (7 mm) hook, ch 17 (15, 15, 15, 13), turn.

Row 1 (RS): Sc in 2nd ch from hook and in each ch to end, turn. Place marker on RS of work (not at edge). [16 (14, 14, 14, 12) sts]

INCREASING FOR SIDE OF SLEEVE

Row 2 (WS): Ch 2 (count as hdc), hdc in next and each sc across to last st, 2 hdc in last st, turn. [17 (15, 15, 15, 13) sts]

Row 3: Ch 8, sc in 2nd ch from hook, sc in each of next 6 chs (count as 7 sc), sc in blo of next and each hdc across to last st, sc in last st, turn. [24 (22, 22, 22, 20) sts]

Row 4: Ch 2 (count as hdc), hdc in next and each sc across to last st, 2 hdc in last st, turn. [25 (23, 23, 23, 21) sts]

Row 5: Ch 6, sc in 2nd ch from hook, sc in each of next 4 chs (count as 5 sc), sc in blo of each hdc across to tch, sc in tch, turn. [30 (28, 28, 28, 26) sts]

Rep last 2 rows 3 more times. [48 (46, 46, 46, 44) sts]

Place marker. Work even in pat as established until 10" from this marker, ending with pat row 2 completed.

DECREASING FOR OPPOSITE SIDE OF SLEEVE

Next Row (WS): Ch 2 (count as hdc), hdc in next and each st to last 7 sts, sc2tog, turn. Rem 5 sts unworked. [42 (40, 40, 40, 38) sts]

Next Row: As pat row 2.

Rep last 2 rows 3 more times. [24 (22, 22, 22, 20) sts]

Next Row: Ch 2 (count as hdc), hdc in each st across to last 9 sts, sc2tog, turn. Rem 7 sts unworked. [16 (14, 14, 14, 12) sts]

Next Row: As pat row 2. Fasten off.

Collar

With RS tog, sew front to back at right shoulder.

With RS of front facing you and using J/10 (6 mm) hook, join yarn at left shoulder.

Next Row: Ch 3 (count as dc), 8 dc down left front of neck, 10 dc across center front of neck, 8 dc up right front of neck, and 20 dc across back of neck, turn. [46 dc]

Next Row: Ch 3, *FPDC in next dc, BPDC in next dc*, rep from * to * to last st, dc in last st, turn.

Next Row: Ch 3, *FPDC in next dc in row below, BPDC in next dc in row below*, rep from * to * to last st, dc in last st, turn.

Rep last row until collar is 3" deep, change to K/10.5 (7 mm) hook, and cont rep as established until 6" from beg of collar. Fasten off.

With RS tog, join collar ends for 3" from base of neck. Refold collar so WS of collar ends are tog. Sew tog to end of collar.

With RS tog, sew front to back at left shoulder.

Front Waistband

With RS facing you and using J/10 (6 mm) hook, join yarn at corner of bottom edge.

Row 1: Ch 3 (count as dc), dc in ends of every row along bottom edge of front, turn. [38 (42, 46, 50, 54) dc]

Row 2: Ch 3 (count as dc), *FPDC in next dc, BPDC in next dc*, rep from * to * to last st, dc in last st, turn.

Row 3: Ch 3 (count as dc), *FPDC in next st in row below, BPDC in next st in row below*, rep from * to * to last st, dc in last st. Fasten off.

Back Waistband

Work as for front waistband.

Sleeve Edging

With RS facing you and using J/10 (6 mm) hook, join yarn at corner of bottom edge.

Row 1: Ch 3 (count as dc), dc in end of every row along bottom edge of sleeve, turn. [20 dc]

Work front waistband row 2 twice. Fasten off.

Make cuff for rem sleeve in same manner.

Finishing

Place marker on front, 10" down from outer end of right shoulder seam, to mark armhole. Also place marker 10" below left shoulder seam on front. Mark back in same manner. With RS tog, sew front and back tog at side seams.

Fold a sleeve in half along its length, RS tog, aligning underarm edges. Sew these edges tog to make underarm seam. Turn sleeve RS out. Then slide sleeve into body until it's at an armhole. Align underarm and side seams, and match edge of sleeve with edge of armhole. Sew the edges together. Rep to make, insert, and join rem sleeve to body. Remove markers.

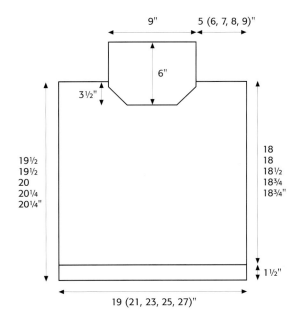

FRONT

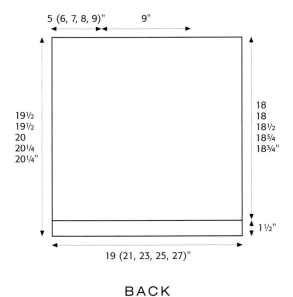

BACK

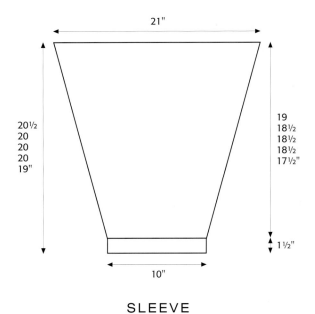

SLEEVE

Ins and Outs

BY TOSCA J. MARK

Y ou won't find many sweaters as elegant—or as easy to create—as this one. The luxurious, finished fabric begins with a humble mesh pattern made with chain and double-crochet stitches. Then the mesh is beautifully embellished by weaving a doubled strand of yarn vertically through the crocheted rows.

DESIGN DETAILS

- Semiloose to loose fitting
- Body length below high hip
- Neckline rests on collarbone
- Filet background and edging in main color

FEATURED STITCHES

Chain (ch); see page 99

Chain-space (ch-sp); see page 111

Double crochet (dc); see page 103

Double crochet 2 together (dc2tog); see page 112

Single crochet (sc); see page 100

Single crochet 2 together (sc2tog); see page 111

Slip stitch (sl st); see page 102

SIZING

To fit bust: 31½ (34¼, 37¼, 41, 43¼)"

Finished bust: 37½ (40½, 43½, 47, 50)"

MATERIALS

4 (4, 4, 5, 5) balls of Red Heart *Soft* (100% acrylic: 5 ozs./140 g; 328 yds./295 m); #7760 Cranberry (MC)

2 balls of Bernat *Illusions* (90% acrylic, 10% nylon: 5 ozs./140 g; 195 yds./113 m); #606 Gemstone *or* 1 ball of Bernat *Mirage* (90% acrylic, 10% nylon: 10 ozs./280 g; 390 yds./350 m); #706 Gemstone (A)

G/6 (4.25 mm) crochet hook

Size 7 (4.5 mm) crochet hook

4 stitch markers

GAUGE

17 sts and 10 rows to 4" in Filet pattern, with size 7 (4.5 mm) hook. Measure gauge swatch before weaving strands through rows.

FILET PATTERN

Multiple of 2 sts (add 3 sts for base chain)

Foundation Row (RS): Dc in 6th ch from hook (count as dc and ch-1 sp), *ch 1, sk 1 ch, dc in next ch*, rep from * to * to end, turn.

Row 1: Ch 4 (count as dc and ch-1 sp), dc in next dc, *ch 1, sk 1 ch-sp, dc in next dc*, rep from * to * to end, making last dc in 2nd ch from top of tch, turn.

Rep row 1.

NOTE: *The end-of-row stitch counts provided in the instructions that follow list only the number of double crochet stitches because they're easy to count.*

Front

With MC and size 7 (4.5 mm) hook, ch 88 (94, 100, 108, 116).

Row 1: Dc in 6th ch from hook (count as dc and ch-1 sp), *ch 1, sk 1 ch, dc in next ch*, rep from * to * to end, turn. [43 (46, 49, 53, 57) dc]

Row 2: As Filet pat row 1.

Rep last row until 16½ (16½, 18¼, 18¼, 18¼)" from beg.

RIGHT SHOULDER SHAPING

Next Row (Dec Row 1): Ch 4 (count as dc and ch-sp), dc in next dc, *ch 1, dc in next dc*, rep from * to * 13 (14, 15, 17, 18) more times, ch 1, dc2tog (sk ch-sp between last 2 dc), turn. Rem 25 (27, 29, 31, 34) dc unworked.

Next Row (Dec Row 2): Ch 3, sk 1 ch-sp, sk 1 dc, sk 1 ch-sp, dc in next dc, *ch 1, dc in next dc*, rep from * to * to end, turn. [15 (16, 17, 19, 20) dc]

Next Row (Dec Row 3): Ch 4 (count as dc and ch-sp), dc in next dc, *ch 1, dc in next dc*, rep from * to * 10 (11, 12, 14, 15) more times, ch 1, dc2tog (sk ch-sp between last 2 dc, don't count dec row 2 tch as dc), turn. [14 (15, 16, 18, 19) dc]

Next Row (Dec Row 4): As dec row 2. [12 (13, 14, 16, 17) dc]

Work 4 rows even in pat as established. Fasten off.

LEFT SHOULDER SHAPING

Next Row: With RS facing you and working into last full row, sk 8 (9, 10, 10, 12) dc (for neckline). Attach yarn in top of next dc, ch 4 (count as dc and ch-1 sp), dc in next dc, *ch 1, dc in next dc*, rep from * to * to end, turn. [17 (18, 19, 21, 22) dc]

Next Row: Ch 4 (count as dc and ch-sp), dc in next dc, *ch 1, dc in next dc*, rep from * to * 11 (12, 13, 15, 16) more times, ch 1, dc2tog (sk ch-sp between last 2 dc), turn. Rem st unworked. [15 (16, 17, 19, 20) dc]

Next Row: As dec row 2 for right shoulder shaping. [13 (14, 15, 17, 18) dc]

Next Row: Ch 4 (count as dc and ch-sp), dc in next dc, *ch 1, dc in next dc*, rep from * to * 8 (9, 10, 12, 13) more times, dc2tog (sk ch-sp between last 2 dc), turn. [12 (13, 14, 16, 17) dc]

Work 4 rows even in pat as established. Fasten off.

Back

Work as for front to right shoulder shaping.

Work 2 rows even in pat.

RIGHT SHOULDER SHAPING

Work as for right shoulder shaping for front, dec rows 1, 2, 3, and 4.

Work 2 rows even in pat as established. Fasten off.

LEFT SHOULDER SHAPING

Work as for left shoulder shaping for front, EXCEPT work only 2 rows (not 4) even in pat at end of instructions. Fasten off.

Sleeve (Make 2)

With MC and size 7 (4.5 mm) hook, ch 52 (52, 54, 54, 54).

Row 1: Dc in 6th ch from hook (count as dc and ch-1 sp), *ch 1, sk 1 ch, dc in next ch*, rep from * to * to end, turn. [25 (25, 26, 26, 26) dc]

Rows 2 and 3: As Filet pat row 1.

Row 4: Ch 4, dc in base of tch, work in pat to last st, (dc, ch 1, dc) in last st, turn. [27 (27, 28, 28, 28) dc]

Work 2 rows even in pat.

Rep row 4 once. [29 (29, 30, 30, 30) dc]

Rep last 3 rows until sleeve is 43 (43, 44, 48, 48) dc wide.

Work even until 17½ (18, 18½, 19, 19½)" from beg. Fasten off.

Weaving

Cut a 62 (62, 62, 64, 66)" strand of A. Fold in half. Wrap folded end around first ch-1 sp at bottom of front. Pull yarn ends through fold to secure; then thread both ends on a tapestry needle. Using the illustration as a guide, weave doubled yarn loosely up through rows, from bottom to top, moving needle in and out through the rows of the filet background.

After weaving, check length of body to make sure you haven't shortened it by weaving too tightly. Loosen weaving if necessary.

Pull one strand out of needle. With WS facing you, weave strand still on needle back and forth through the WS of a nearby dc post. Rethread rem yarn strand, and rep. Trim loose ends.

Secure new strand A to ch-1 sp at top of front, in next column. Weave the doubled strand in and out of the rows, this time from top to bottom. Weave in ends as before.

Cont weaving the filet background in this manner, alternating start of each strand between top and bottom.

Weave remaining garment pieces in same manner. Use 58 (60, 61, 62, 63)" strand lengths for sleeves.

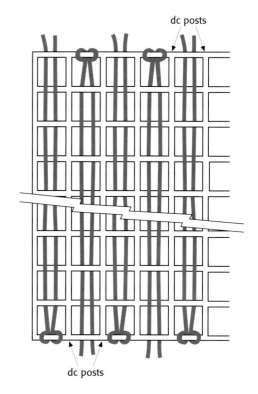

WS OF FILET BACKGROUND WITH STRANDS WOVEN THROUGH

Finishing

With RS tog, sew front to back at shoulders.

Spread joined, opened front and back flat on a table, with RS facing you. Place markers along each edge, 9½ (9½, 10½, 11, 11)" from shoulder seams, to mark armholes. Position sleeve across joined pieces, RS down, with wider end between markers on one side and aligned with edge of armhole. Sew sleeve to body. Attach rem sleeve in same manner.

Remove markers. Refold body and sleeves, RS tog, aligning all matching edges. Join front to back by sewing up sides and along sleeve underarms. Join rem side in same manner.

NECKLINE EDGING

With RS facing you, attach MC at left shoulder seam, using G/6 (4.25 mm) hook.

Rnd 1: Ch 1, sc in each dc and ch-1 sp around neckline.

Rnd 2: Ch 1, sc in first and each st to end, sl st in first ch-1 sp to close rnd.

Rep last rnd 3 more times. Fasten off.

WAISTBAND EDGING

With RS facing you, attach MC at left side seam by using G/6 (4.25 mm) hook.

Rnd 1: Ch 1, sc in each dc and ch-1 sp around bottom edge.

Rnd 2: Ch 1, sc in first and each st to end, sl st in first ch-1 sp to close rnd.

Rep last rnd 3 more times.

Next Rnd: Ch 1, sc around, AT SAME TIME dec 30 sts by working evenly spaced sc2tog. Fasten off.

SLEEVE EDGING

With RS facing you, attach MC at underarm seam by using G/6 (4.25 mm) hook.

Rnds 1 and 2: As rnds 1 and 2 of waistband edging.

Rnds 3 and 4: As rnd 2 of waistband edging.

Rnd 5: Ch 1, sc around, AT SAME TIME dec 18 sts by working evenly spaced sc2tog. Fasten off.

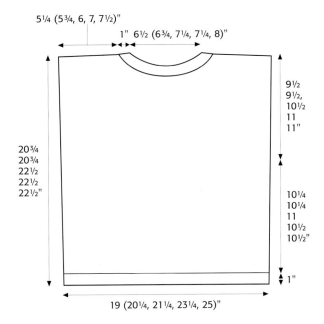

5¼ (5¾, 6, 7, 7½)"

1" 6½ (6¾, 7¼, 7¼, 8)"

9½
9½,
10½
11
11"

20¾
20¾
22½
22½
22½"

10¼
10¼
11
10½
10½"

1"

19 (20¼, 21¼, 23¼, 25)"

BACK

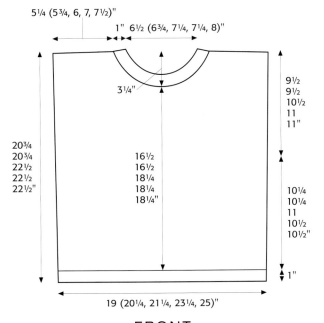

5¼ (5¾, 6, 7, 7½)"

1" 6½ (6¾, 7¼, 7¼, 8)"

3¼"

9½
9½
10½
11
11"

20¾
20¾
22½
22½
22½"

16½
16½
18¼
18¼
18¼"

10¼
10¼
11
10½
10½"

1"

19 (20¼, 21¼, 23¼, 25)"

FRONT

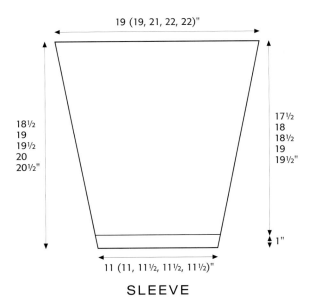

19 (19, 21, 22, 22)"

18½
19
19½
20
20½"

17½
18
18½
19
19½"

1"

11 (11, 11½, 11½, 11½)"

SLEEVE

Tokyo Vest

By Nancy Nehring

*F*or a subtle hint of Asia, try this exotic vest. The pattern is an excellent one for beginners because neither the length nor the shoulder width is critical, and if the waist is too loose or tight, reworking the small side panels is easy and quick. (These rectangular panels, made in a second color, join the front pieces to the back.)

DESIGN DETAILS

- Semifitted
- Side panels end at waist
- Body length to approx 3" below waist
- Wide front band narrows around neck to form stand-up collar
- Short rows (entire row not worked) increase front band width

FEATURED STITCHES

Chain (ch); see page 99
Double crochet (dc); see page 103
Half double crochet (hdc); see page 103
Single crochet (sc); see page 100
Slip stitch (sl st); see page 102

SIZING

To fit bust: 31½ (34¼, 37¼, 41, 43¼)"
Finished chest (top of side panel): 34¼ (36, 39½, 41¾, 43¼)"

MATERIALS

5 (5, 5, 6, 6) skeins of Skacel *Paradiso* (60% cotton, 30% acrylic, 10% nylon: 1¾ ozs./50 g; 110 yds./100 m); Color #04 (MC)
4 (4, 4, 4, 4) skeins of Skacel *Fortissima* (75% cotton, 25% nylon: 1¾ ozs./50 g; 231 yds./210 m); #02 Black (A)
F/5 (4 mm) crochet hook
I/9 (5.5 mm) crochet hook
Three ⅝" plastic rings
2" x 4" strip of thin cardboard
Black sewing thread
Hand-sewing needle

GAUGE

16 dc and 8 rows to 4", with I/9 (5.5 mm) hook and MC
20 sc and 32 rows to 4", with F/5 (4 mm) hook and A

NOTE: *In the following instructions, when the turning chain counts as a stitch, work the last stitch of each row into the top of the turning chain of the previous row unless the instructions indicate otherwise. Don't work the first stitch of a row into the base of the turning chain unless told to make an increase.*

Front Panel (Make 2)

With MC and I/9 (5.5 mm) hook, ch 15 (16, 17, 18, 19).

Row 1: Dc in 3rd ch from hook (count as 2 dc), dc in each ch to end, turn. [13 (14, 15, 16, 17) dc]

Row 2: Ch 3 (count as dc), dc in next and each st to end, turn.

Rep last row until 18 (18, 19, 19, 20)" from beg.

Next Row: Ch 1, sl st in first 4 sts, sc in each of next 3 (4, 4, 4, 5) sts, hdc in each of next 3 (3, 4, 4, 4) sts, dc in each of next 3 (3, 3, 4, 4) sts, turn. [9 (10, 11, 12, 13) sts]

Next Row: Ch 3 (count as dc), dc in each of next 3 (3, 3, 4, 4) dc, hdc in each of next 3 (3, 4, 4, 4) hdc, sc in each of next 3 (4, 4, 4, 5) sc. Fasten off.

RIGHT PANEL EDGING

With RS facing you, attach A to bottom corner, using F/5 (4 mm) hook.

Rnd 1: Ch 1, *2 sc in first st, sc in flo of next st*, rep from * to * across bottom to corner, 3 sc in corner, 3 sc in each dc up side, 3 sc in corner, **2 sc in next st, 1 sc in next st (through both lps)**, rep from ** to ** across shoulder, 3 sc in corner, 3 sc in each dc down rem side, 3 sc in corner, sl st to join to first st in rnd.

Rnd 2: Ch 1, sc in each st to end, AT SAME TIME working 3 sc in each corner.

Rep last rnd 2 more times. Fasten off.

LEFT PANEL EDGING

As for right panel edging, EXCEPT begin stitching up the side, cont across shoulder, down rem side, and across bottom.

Back

With MC and I/9 (5.5 mm) hook, ch 51 (54, 58, 61, 65).

Row 1: Dc in 3rd ch from hook (count as 2 dc), dc in each ch to end, turn. [49 (52, 56, 59, 63) dc]

Row 2: Ch 3 (count as dc), dc in each st to end, turn.

Rep last row until 18 (18, 19, 19, 20)" from beg, ending with WS row completed.

RIGHT SHOULDER SHAPING

Next Row (RS): Ch 1, sl st in first 4 sts, sc in next 3 (4, 4, 4, 5) sts, hdc in next 3 (3, 4, 4, 4) sts, dc in next 3 (3, 3, 4, 4) sts, turn. Rem 36 (38, 41, 43, 46) sts unworked.

Next Row: Ch 3 (count as dc), dc in next 2 (2, 2, 3, 3) dc, hdc in next 3 (3, 4, 4, 4) hdc, sc in next 3 (4, 4, 4, 5) sc. Fasten off.

LEFT SHOULDER SHAPING

Using I/9 (5.5 mm) hook and with WS facing you, attach MC to corner, on last full-length row.

Work as for right shoulder shaping. Center 23 (24, 26, 27, 29) sts unworked. Fasten off.

EDGING

Using F/5 (4 mm) hook and with WS facing you, attach A to bottom right corner. (The first round is worked all around the edges of this garment piece.)

Rnd 1 (Bottom): *2 sc in first st, sc through flo in next st*, rep from * to * to opposite corner, 3 sc in corner, pivot work.

Rnd 1 (Left Side): 3 sc in each dc, 3 sc in corner, pivot work.

Rnd 1 (Left Shoulder): Rep from * to * (as for rnd 1 bottom) to next corner, 3 sc in corner, pivot work.

Rnd 1 (Neckline): Rep from * to * (as for rnd 1 bottom) to inner corner of neckline, sk 1 st, rep from * to * to opposite inner corner, sk 1 st, rep from * to * to inner corner of right shoulder, 3 sc in corner, pivot work.

Rnd 1 (Right Shoulder): As for left shoulder.

Rnd 1 (Right Side): As for left side, join to start of rnd with sl st.

Rnd 2: Sc in each st, EXCEPT make 3 sc in each outer corner and sk 1 st at inner corners of neckline.

Rep last rnd 2 more times. Fasten off.

Side Panel (Make 2)

With A and F/5 (4 mm) hook, ch 22 (24, 26, 28, 30).

Row 1: Sc in 2nd ch from hook, sc in each ch to end, turn. [21 (23, 25, 27, 29) sc]

Row 2: Ch 1, sc in first and each st to end, turn.

Rep last row until 6¾" from beg. Fasten off.

Finishing

With WS tog, place front panel on top of back, and sc shoulders tog, using A and F/5 (4 mm) hook. With WS tog, place bottom edge of side panel 3" above lower edge of corresponding front panel. Join edges with sc. Join rem side panel edge to corresponding side of back. In same manner, sc rem side panel to rem front panel and opposite edge of back.

FRONT/NECK BAND

With RS facing you and using F/5 (4 mm) hook, attach A to lower corner of right front.

Row 1: Ch 1, sc in each st up edge of front until even with bottom edge of the 4th row down from the shoulder of MC, sl st in next st, turn.

Rows 2, 4, 6, 8, 10, and 12: Ch 1, sk sl st, sc in next st, sc in each st to bottom edge, turn.

Row 3: As row 1, EXCEPT sc until even with bottom edge of 7th row below shoulder of MC.

Row 5: As row 1, EXCEPT sc until even with bottom edge of 10th row.

Row 7: As row 1, EXCEPT sc until even with bottom edge of 13th row.

Row 9: As row 1, EXCEPT sc until even with bottom edge of 16th row.

Row 11: As row 1, EXCEPT sc until even with bottom edge of 19th row.

Row 13: Sc in each st up right front, sk 1 st at each inside corner where shoulder meets back neck, sc in each st to lower edge of left front, turn.

Rows 14–25: Working on left front, rep rows 1–12.

Working up left front, around neck, and down right front, rep row 13.

Cont working sc around entire front/neck band as established 3 (3, 5, 7, 9) more times. Fasten off.

Button (Make 3)

To make each button, follow the instructions in
  "Crocheted Buttons and Frogs" (see page 62). Use
  A and a F/5 (4 mm) hook.

Frog (Make 3 sets)

Each of the 3 frogs consists of 2 separate pieces. To make
  these 6 pieces, follow the instructions in "Crocheted
  Buttons and Frogs" (see page 62) and use A and an
  F/5 (4 mm) hook.

ATTACHING FROGS AND BUTTONS

Overlap right front 1" over left front. Position larger frog
  piece on right front, with edge of right front band
  running through center of largest loop. Place smaller
  frog section on left front band. Sew frog pieces to vest
  through the Vs on their decorative loops, leaving large
  loop on larger frog piece free to accept button. Sew
  button on top of smaller frog piece on left front band,
  where 3 loops overlap. Rep to attach rem frog pieces
  and buttons.

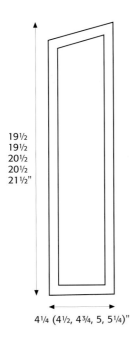

19½
19½
20½
20½
21½"

4¼ (4½, 4¾, 5, 5¼)"

FRONT PANEL

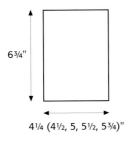

6¾"

4¼ (4½, 5, 5½, 5¾)"

SIDE PANEL

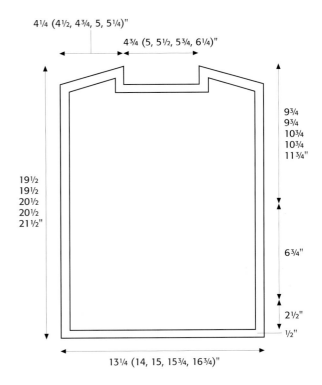

4¼ (4½, 4¾, 5, 5¼)"

4¾ (5, 5½, 5¾, 6¼)"

9¾
9¾
10¾
10¾
11¾"

19½
19½
20½
20½
21½"

6¾"

2½"

½"

13¼ (14, 15, 15¾, 16¾)"

BACK

F O U N D A T I O N S

CROCHETED BUTTONS AND FROGS

Nancy Nehring, the guru of crocheted closures, developed this wonderfully simple method for making crocheted buttons and frogs.

Start each button by completely covering a ⁵/₈" plastic ring with about sixty single crochet stitches. (The number of stitches depends on your hook size and yarn.) Fasten off the thread, leaving a 6"-long tail.

Next, thread the tail on a needle, and weave it in and out of the Vs formed by the two loops at the top of each single crochet. Then push the Vs to one side of the ring, pull the tail tight, and tie a knot. You can use the rest of the tail to sew the button onto the garment.

Each frog consists of two separate parts: one for the left front of the garment and one for the right. Since the right front overlaps the left on women's garments, the right-front frog piece must be larger than the one on the left so that it will fit over its corresponding button.

To make each larger frog piece, wrap yarn three times around the 4" length of a 2" x 4" piece of cardboard, and tie together the loose ends. Slide the yarn off the cardboard, and single crochet around the circumference of the looped circle of yarn about sixty times, joining the ends of the round with a slip stitch. Fasten off.

Using the photograph above as a guide, twist the crocheted circle into four loops, making one loop slightly larger than the others so that it will fit over a button. Twist the tops of the single crochet stitches to the outer edges of each loop. With a sewing needle and thread, secure the loops by sewing through the center, where they overlap.

Make each smaller frog piece for the left front in the same fashion, but wrap the yarn around the 2" width of the cardboard strip, work only forty single crochets around the circle of yarn, and shape only three loops. As you shift the top of each single crochet to the outside of each loop, you may need to twist the stitch; just hide the twisted parts at the center, under one of the lower loops.

Summer Breeze

BY NANCY BROWN

*U*nlike sweaters for warm-weather wear that provide comfort at the expense of modesty, this wonderful little top includes an openwork pattern to keep you cool and a bodice pattern that guarantees full coverage. Don't be intimidated by the stitches, subtle details, and shaping; they're not difficult to master.

DESIGN DETAILS

- Fitted bodice with cutaway front
- Body length to high hip
- Set-in short sleeve ends just above elbow

FEATURED STITCHES

Chain (ch); see page 99

Chain-space (ch-sp); see page 111

Double crochet (dc); see page 103

Double crochet 2 together (dc2tog); see page 112

Single crochet (sc); see page 100

Single crochet 2 together (sc2tog); see page 111

Slip stitch (sl st); see page 102

SIZING

To fit bust: 31½ (34¼, 37¼, 41, 43¼)"

Finished bust: 35 (38, 42, 45, 47)"

MATERIALS

7 (7, 8, 9, 9) balls of Skacel *Riviera* (45% cotton, 30% linen, 25% rayon: 1¾ ozs./50 g; 110 yds./100 m); Color #24

H/8 (5 mm) crochet hook

I/9 (5.5 mm) crochet hook

8 stitch markers

Five ⅝" buttons

GAUGE

16 sts and 12 rows to 4" in Griddle pattern, with I/9 (5.5 mm) hook

MESH PATTERN

Multiple of 2 sts + 1 st (add 3 sts for base chain)

Foundation Row (RS): Dc in 6th ch from hook (count tch as dc and ch-1 sp), *ch 1, sk 1 ch, dc in next ch*, rep from * to * to end, turn.

Row 1: Ch 4 (count tch as dc and ch-1 sp), *dc in next dc, ch 1, sk 1 ch*, rep from * to * to tch, dc in 2nd ch from top of tch, turn.

Rep row 1.

To Dec 1 Dc at Beg and End of Row: Ch 4 (count as dc and ch-1 sp), sk first dc (the one the tch is built on), dc2tog over next 2 dc (sk ch-1 sp between), work in pat across to last 3 dc, dc2tog over next 2 dc (sk ch-1 sp between), ch 1, dc in 2nd ch from top of tch, turn.

GRIDDLE PATTERN

NOTE: *Don't count the turning chain at the start of each row as a stitch. In other words, make the first stitch of the row into the first stitch of the previous row, which is directly underneath.*

Multiple of 2 sts (add 1 st for base chain)

Foundation Row: Sc in 2nd ch from hook, *dc in next ch, sc in next ch*, rep from * to * to last ch, dc in last ch, turn.

Row 1: Ch 1, sc in first dc, dc in next sc, *sc in next dc, dc in next sc*, rep from * to * to end, working last dc in last st of previous row (not tch), turn.

Rep row 1.

To Inc 1 St at End of Row: Ch 1, sc in first dc, dc in next sc, *sc in next dc, dc in next sc*, rep from * to * across to last st and tch, sc in last st, dc in tch (1 inc made), turn.

Back

With I/9 (5.5 mm) hook, chain 74 (78, 84, 92, 96).

Row 1 (RS): Dc in 6th ch from hook (count tch as dc and ch-1 sp), *ch 1, sk 1 ch, dc in next ch*, rep from * to * to end, turn. [36 (38, 41, 45, 47) dc]

Place marker on RS.

Row 2: As Mesh pat row 1. [36 (38, 41, 45, 47) dc]

Rep last row 6 more times.

Next Row (Griddle Pat Set-Up): Ch 1, sc in first dc (base of tch), *sc around next ch-1 sp, dc in next dc*, rep from * to * to tch, sc around tch, dc in 3rd ch from base of tch, turn. [71 (75, 81, 89, 93) sts]

Next Row: As Griddle pat, inc 1 st at end of row. [72 (76, 82, 90, 94) sts]

Next Row: As Griddle pat row 1, turn.

Rep last row until 10½ (10½, 10½, 10¾, 10½)" from beg, ending with WS row completed. Fasten off.

ARMHOLE SHAPING

Next Row (RS): Reattach yarn with sc in 7th (7th, 8th, 9th, 9th) st, work in Griddle pat as established across next 59 (63, 67, 73, 77) sts, turn. Rem 6 (6, 7, 8, 8) sts unworked. [60 (64, 68, 74, 78) sts]

Next Row: Ch 1, sc2tog, work in pat as established to last 2 sts, working sc in top of dc and dc in top of sc, dc2tog, turn. [58 (62, 66, 72, 76) sts]

Rep last row 5 more times. [48 (52, 56, 62, 66) sts]

Large Only

Rep last row 1 more time. [60 sts]

All Sizes

Cont in pat as established on 48 (52, 56, 60, 66) sts until 18½ (19½, 19½, 20, 20½)" from beg (this is approx 2 rows less than desired length).

RIGHT SHOULDER SHAPING

Next Row (RS): Work in pat as established across 11 (13, 13, 15, 15) sts, dc2tog, turn. Rem 35 (37, 41, 43, 47) sts unworked.

Next Row: Work in pat to end. Fasten off.

LEFT SHOULDER SHAPING

Next Row (RS): Sk center 22 (22, 26, 26, 32) sts (neckline), reattach yarn in next st with sc, dc2tog, work in pat as established to end, working sc in top of dc and dc in top of sc, turn. [12 (14, 14, 16, 16) sts]

Next Row: Work in pat as established to end. Fasten off.

Left Front

With I/9 (5.5 mm) hook, chain 36 (36, 38, 42, 44).

Row 1 (RS): Dc in 6th ch from hook (count tch as dc and ch-1 sp), *ch 1, sk 1 ch, dc in next ch*, rep from * to * to end, turn. [17 (17, 18, 20, 21) dc]

Rows 2 and 3: As Mesh pat row 1.

Row 4: Ch 4 (count tch as dc and ch-1 sp), dc in base of ch-4 tch just made (inc made), *ch 1, sk 1 ch, dc in next dc*, rep from * to * to tch, ch 1, dc in 2nd ch from top of tch, turn. [18 (18, 19, 21, 22) dc]

Rows 5 and 6: Work even in pat, turn.

X-Small Only

Rows 7 and 8: Work in pat to end, turn.

Small, Medium, Large, and X-Large Only

Row 7: Work in pat across to tch, (dc, ch 1, dc) in 2nd ch from top of tch (inc made), turn. [(19, 20, 22, 23) dc]

Row 8: Work in pat to end, turn.

All Sizes

Next Row: As Griddle pat set-up for back. [35 (37, 39, 43, 45) sts]

Next Row: As Griddle pat, inc 1 st at end of row. [36 (38, 40, 44, 46) sts]

Next Row: As Griddle pat row 1, turn.

Rep last row until same length as back to armhole shaping, ending at armhole edge. Fasten off.

ARMHOLE SHAPING

Next Row (RS): Reattach yarn with sc in 7th (7th, 9th, 9th, 9th) st, work in Griddle pat as established to end, turn. [30 (32, 32, 36, 38) sts]

Next Row: Work in pat as established to last 2 sts, dc2tog (dec made), turn. [29 (31, 31, 35, 37) sts]

Next Row: Ch 1, sc2tog (dec made), work in pat as established to end, turn. [28 (30, 30, 34, 36) sts]

Rep last 2 rows 2 more times. [24 (26, 26, 30, 32) sts]

Work even in pat until 15¼ (16, 16, 16, 16)" from beg, ending at sleeve edge.

NECK SHAPING

Next Row (RS; Dec Row 1): Place marker. Work 15 (17, 19, 21, 21) sts in Griddle pat as established, dc2tog (dec made), turn. Rem 7 (7, 5, 7, 9) sts unworked. [16 (18, 20, 22, 22) sts]

Next Row: Work in pat as established to end, turn.

Next Row (Dec Row 2): Ch 1, sc2tog (dec made), work in pat as established to last 2 sts, dc2tog (dec made), turn. [14 (16, 18, 20, 20) sts]

Rep last row 1 more time. [12 (14, 16, 18, 18) sts]

Work 1 row even.

Medium, Large, and X-Large Only

Next Row: As dec row 2. [(14, 16, 16) sts]

All Sizes

Work even in pat as established until same length as back. Fasten off.

Right Front

Work as for left front to armhole shaping, rev shaping by making mesh inc at end of rows rather than beg (work in pat as established to end of row, working last dc in top of tch, ch 1, dc in top of tch). See "Shaping—and Reversing Shaping" on page 74. End at front edge. (WS row completed.)

ARMHOLE SHAPING

Next Row (RS): Work even in Griddle pat across 30 (32, 32, 36, 38) sts, turn. Rem 6 (6, 8, 8, 8) sts unworked.

Work as for left front armhole shaping, rev shaping and ending at front edge. Fasten off. [24 (26, 26, 30, 32) sts]

NECK SHAPING

Next Row (RS): Reattach yarn with sc in 8th (8th, 6th, 8th, 10th) st, place marker, ch 1, sc2tog, work in pat as established to end, turn. [16 (18, 20, 22, 22) sts]

Work as for left front neck, rev shaping. Fasten off.

Sleeve (Make 2)

With I/9 (5.5 mm) hook, ch 54 (54, 58, 62, 66).

Row 1 (RS): Dc in 6th ch from hook (count as dc and ch-1 sp), *ch 1, sk 1 ch, dc in next ch*, rep from * to * to end, turn. [26 (26, 28, 30, 32) dc]

Row 2: Ch 4 (count tch as dc and ch-1 sp), work even in Mesh pat to end, turn.

Row 3: Ch 4 (count as dc and ch-1 sp), dc in base of tch just made (inc made), *ch 1, sk 1 st, dc in next dc*, rep from * to * to tch, ch 1, (dc, ch 1, dc) in 2nd ch from top of tch, turn. [28 (28, 30, 32, 34) dc]

Row 4: Work even in pat, turn.

Row 5: As row 3. [30 (30, 32, 34, 36) dc]

Row 6: Work even in pat. Fasten off.

CAP SHAPING

Follow instructions for your size.

X-Small, Small, and Medium Only

Row 7 (RS): Reattach yarn in 5th dc from edge, ch 4 (count as dc and ch-1 sp), work in pat across to last 4 dc, turn. [22 (22, 24) dc]

Work 3 rows in pat, dec 1 dc at beg and end of row (see "Mesh Pattern" on page 64). [16 (16, 18) dc]

Work 1 row even in pat, turn.

X-Small Only

Row 12: Work in pat, dec 1 dc at beg and end of row. [14 dc]

Row 13: Work in pat to end, turn.

Rep row 12 two more times. Work 1 row even in pat. Fasten off. [10 dc]

Small Only

Row 12: Work in pat, dec 1 dc at beg and end of row. [14 dc]

Row 13: Work in pat to end, turn.

Rep last 2 rows 2 more times. Fasten off. [10 dc]

Medium Only

Row 12: Work in pat to end, turn.

Row 13: Work in pat, dec 1 dc at beg and end of row. [16 dc]

Row 14: Work in pat to end, turn.

Rep last 2 rows 2 more times. Fasten off. [12 dc]

Large and X-Large Only

Row 7 (RS): Reattach yarn in 5th dc from edge, ch 4 (count as dc and ch-1 sp), work in pat across to last 4 dc, turn. [(24, 26) dc]

Row 8: Work even in pat.

Rows 9 and 10: Work in pat, dec 1 dc at beg and end of row. [(20, 22) dc]

Row 11: Work even in pat.

Rep last 2 rows 4 more times. [(12, 14) dc]

Large Only

Fasten off.

X-Large Only

Row 20: Work in pat to end. Fasten off.

Finishing

With RS tog, sew fronts to back at shoulder and side seams.

Fold a sleeve in half along its length, RS tog, aligning underarm edges. Sew these edges tog to make underarm seam. Turn sleeve RS out. Then slide sleeve into body until it's at an armhole. Align underarm and side seams, and match edge of sleeve with edge of armhole. Sew the edges together. Rep to make, insert, and join rem sleeve.

BUTTON BAND

Follow instructions for your size.

X-Small and Small Only

Row 1: With H/8 (5 mm) hook and RS of left front facing you, join yarn with sc at stitch marker at start of neck shaping, work evenly spaced sc down front edge to uppermost row of Griddle pat, turn.

Row 2: Ch 1, work 1 sc in each st to end. Fasten off. Place markers in desired locations for buttons.

Medium, Large, and X-Large Only

Row 1: With H/8 (5 mm) hook and WS of left front facing you, join yarn with sc and work 1 row of sc evenly spaced from first row of Griddle pat (at waist) to marker for neck shaping, turn.

Rows 2 and 3: Ch 1, work 1 sc in each st to end. Fasten off. Place markers in desired locations for buttons.

BUTTONHOLE BAND

Follow instructions for your size.

X-Small and Small Only

Row 1: With H/8 (5 mm) hook and RS of right front facing you, join yarn with sc and work 1 row of sc as for button band, but starting from first row of Griddle pat (at waist), turn.

Row 2: Ch 1, work 1 sc in each st to end, working (ch 1, sk 1) to make buttonhole that corresponds with marker on button band. Fasten off.

Medium, Large, and X-Large Only

Row 1: With H/8 (5 mm) hook and WS of right front facing you, join yarn with sc and work 1 row of sc as for button band, but start at neck shaping marker and end at first row of Griddle pat, turn.

Row 2: Ch 1, work 1 sc in each st to end.

Row 3: Work 1 sc in each st to end, working (ch 1, sk 1) to make buttonhole that corresponds with marker on button band. Fasten off.

EDGING

Rnd 1: With H/8 (5 mm) hook and RS facing you, join yarn at right side seam, and sc around all of the garment edges. The goal is to add enough evenly spaced sc along the edges to keep the work flat. In some cases—corners, for example—you may need to work more than 1 stitch, or inc the space between adjacent sc for a smooth edge. Make these decisions as you stitch. At end of work, join to first st with sl st.

Rnd 2: Ch 1, *sc in next sc, sk 1 st, 3 dc in next st, sk 1 st*, rep from * to * to end of rnd. Fasten off.

Sew on buttons.

SLEEVE EDGING

With H/8 (5 mm) hook and RS facing you, join yarn at sleeve seam and work as for edging. Fasten off.

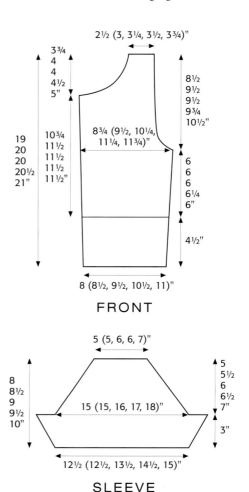

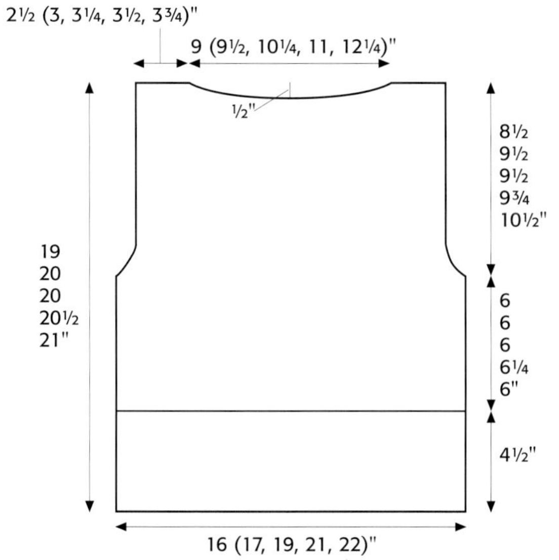

2½ (3, 3¼, 3½, 3¾)"

3¾
4
4
4½
5"

8½
9½
9½
9¾
10½"

19
20
20
20½
21"

10¾
11½
11½
11½
11½"

8¾ (9½, 10¼, 11¼, 11¾)"

6
6
6
6¼
6"

4½"

8 (8½, 9½, 10½, 11)"

FRONT

2½ (3, 3¼, 3½, 3¾)"

9 (9½, 10¼, 11, 12¼)"

½"

8½
9½
9½
9¾
10½"

19
20
20
20½
21"

6
6
6
6¼
6"

4½"

16 (17, 19, 21, 22)"

BACK

5 (5, 6, 6, 7)"

8
8½
9
9½
10"

15 (15, 16, 17, 18)"

5
5½
6
6½
7"

3"

12½ (12½, 13½, 14½, 15)"

SLEEVE

Out of the Box

By Nancy Rawlinson

*C*hase away the chills in style with this pure wool, zipper-front sweater. Inspired by the classic Chanel jacket, its boxy effect is softened with a subtle, undulating wave pattern that's produced by working alternating groups of single- and double-crochet stitches.

DESIGN DETAILS

- Semifitted
- Body length to high hip
- No shoulder seams (back and fronts worked as one piece)
- Full-length sleeve worked from armhole to cuff
- Slight drop shoulder
- Scallop hem edging

FEATURED STITCHES

Chain (ch); see page 99
Double crochet (dc); see page 103
Single crochet (sc); see page 100
Slip stitch (sl st); see page 102

SIZING

To fit bust: 31½ (34¼, 37¼, 41, 43¼)"
Finished bust: 35½ (39½, 41, 45, 47½)"

MATERIALS

NOTE: *Zippers are commonly sold in even-numbered lengths, but you can special order any length at most fabric stores for a perfect fit. Don't buy the zipper until you've assembled the garment pieces and know the exact length you need.*

5 (5, 6, 6, 7) skeins of Briggs & Little *Heritage* (100% wool: 4 ozs./113 g; 215 yds./196 m); #62 Green Heather (MC), and 1 skein #16 Black (A)

J/10 (6 mm) crochet hook

16 (16, 18, 18, 18)" separating zipper

1 stitch marker

All-purpose sewing thread to match zipper

Hand-sewing needle

Quilting pins with large plastic or glass heads

GAUGE

12 sts and 11 rows to 4" in Wave pattern

WAVE PATTERN

NOTE: *The ch-1 turning chain doesn't count as a stitch, so work the first stitch of every row into the base of the turning chain. A ch-3 turning chain does count as a stitch. Work the first stitch of the new row into the next stitch of the previous row, only working into the first stitch (the base of the turning chain) when making an increase.*

Multiple of 8 sts (add 1 st for base chain)

Foundation Row: Sc in 2nd ch from hook, sc in each of next 3 sts, dc in each of next 4 sts, *sc in each of next 4 sts, dc in each of next 4 sts*, rep from * to * to end, turn.

Row 1: Ch 1, *sc in each of next 4 sts, dc in each of next 4 sts*, rep from * to * to end, turn.

Rep row 1.

Body (Back)

With MC, ch 55 (61, 63, 69, 73) loosely.

Row 1 (RS): Sc in 2nd ch from hook, sc in each of next 1 (3, 1, 3, 3) chs, dc in each of next 4 chs, *sc in each of next 4 chs, dc in each of next 4 chs*, rep from * to * to end, turn. [54 (60, 62, 68, 72) sts]

Row 2: Ch 1, work in Wave pat (dc in sc and sc in dc) to end, turn.

Place marker on RS. Cont in Wave pat as established, until 9¾ (9¾, 10¾, 10¾, 10¾)" from beg, ending with WS row completed.

ARMHOLE SHAPING

Next Row (RS): Work in pat across to last 4 sts, turn. Rem 4 sts unworked. [50 (56, 58, 64, 68) sts]

Next Row: Ch 3 (count as dc), dc in each of next 3 sc, work in pat (dc in sc and sc in dc) across to last 4 sts, turn. Rem 4 sts unworked. [46 (52, 54, 60, 64) sts]

Work even in pat as established, starting each row with a ch 3 and working dc in sc and sc in dc, until 17 (17, 18, 19, 19)" from beg, ending with RS row completed, turn. Don't break yarn.

LEFT SHOULDER SHAPING

Next Row (WS): Work in pat as established over 12 (14, 14, 16, 20) sts, turn. Rem 34 (38, 40, 44, 44) sts unworked.

Work even in pat as established until 4" from start of left shoulder, ending with RS row completed.

LEFT NECKLINE AND FRONT SHAPING

Next Row (WS): Work in pat as established to end, ch 9 (9, 12, 11, 11), turn.

Next Row: Sc in 2nd ch from hook, sc in each of next 3 (5, 0, 1, 5) chs, dc in each of next 4 chs, *sc in each of next 4 chs, dc in each of next 4 chs*, rep from * to * to end, turn. [20 (22, 25, 26, 30) sts]

Next Row: Ch 3 (count as dc), dc in each of next 3 sc, *sc in each of next 4 dc, dc in each of next 4 sc*, rep from * to * across to last 0 (2, 5, 6, 2) sts, work sc in dc and dc in sc in each st to end.

Work even in pat as established until 56 (56, 56, 62, 62) rows from start of left armhole shaping, ending with WS row completed.

Next Row (RS): Work in pat as established to end, ch 5, turn.

Next Row: Sc in 2nd ch from hook, sc in each of next 3 chs, dc in each of next 4 sc, cont in pat as established to end, turn.

Work even in pat as established until left front length matches back. Fasten off.

RIGHT SHOULDER AND NECKLINE SHAPING

With RS facing you, attach yarn in upper right corner of last full-width row of back.

Work as for left shoulder shaping, and left neckline and front shaping, EXCEPT work on RS of fabric when instructions refer to WS, and on WS of fabric when instructions refer to RS. (In some sizes, the pattern does not start and end with a complete repeat.)

Left Sleeve

Next Row: With RS facing you, attach MC at inner corner of front armhole. Ignore 4-st dec edge. Ch 3 (count as dc), dc in end of next 3 rows, *sc in end of next 4 rows, dc in end of next 4 rows*, rep from * to *

to inner corner at end of back armhole (ignore 4-st dec edge), turn. Pat doesn't end with complete rep in large and X-large. [56 (56, 56, 62, 62) sts]

Work even in Wave pat as established for 10 (12, 12, 14, 14) rows.

Next Row: Dec 1 st in pat as established, work in pat as established to end, turn. [55 (55, 55, 61, 61) sts]

Rep last row 23 more times. [32 (32, 32, 38, 38) sts]

Work even in pat as established until sleeve is 19 (19, 19½, 19½, 19½)" from armhole. Fasten off.

Right Sleeve

Attach MC at inner corner of back armhole. Working from back armhole to front, work as for left sleeve.

Finishing

With RS tog, sew side and sleeve seams. Remove marker.

FRONT AND NECK EDGING

With RS facing you, attach MC at inner bottom corner (center opening) of right front.

Row 1: Sc along right front edge, right neckline, right shoulder, back neck, left shoulder and neckline, and left front edge, AT SAME TIME working 2 sc at each outer corner and sk 1 st at each inner corner. Fasten off.

Row 2 (RS): Attach A and work as row 1, turn.

Row 3 (Left Front; WS): Sl st in each sc along left front. Fasten off at end of edge (start of neckline).

Row 4 (Right Front; WS): Attach A at hem. Work as row 3 for left front.

HEM EDGING

With RS facing you, join A at inner (center front) corner of left front hem.

Row 1: Ch 1, work sc in each sc and dc in each dc (opposite of established Wave pat) across left front, back, and right front, turn.

Row 2: Work even in Wave pat as established, starting with ch-1 if next st is sc or ch-3 if next st is dc. Fasten off.

SLEEVE EDGING

With RS facing you, join A at underarm seam of
    sleeve hem.

Rnd 1: Ch 1, sc in top of each sc and dc in top of each dc
    around dc (opposite of established Wave pat), sl st in
    ch-1 at start of rnd, don't turn.

Rnd 2: Work even in Wave pat as established, starting
    with ch-1 if next st will be a sc or starting with ch-3 if
    next st will be a dc. Fasten off.

ZIPPER

Pin closed zipper under right and left front, with entire
    length of jacket edges touching. Baste zipper in place,
    and remove pins. Check that neckline and hem cor-
    ners are aligned and crocheted fabric isn't drawn in.
    Open zipper. Using hand-sewing needle and matching
    thread, sew each side of zipper to an edge, placing a
    running stitch close to zipper teeth. Make sure the
    slider moves freely. Use a running stitch to sew the
    free edge of the zipper tape to WS of work.

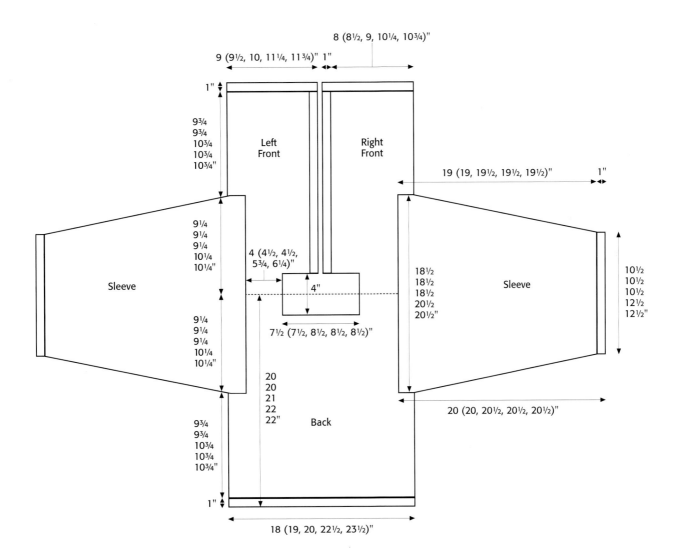

Surf and Turf

BY JANE SNEDDEN PEEVER

*T*his hooded, sleeveless top, with its drawstring-waist styling, looks great worn over *almost any casual outfit, whether you're dressed for a beachside stroll or a family picnic. What's more, you'll be the envy of all your crocheting friends; instructions for attractive crocheted hoods are few and far between.*

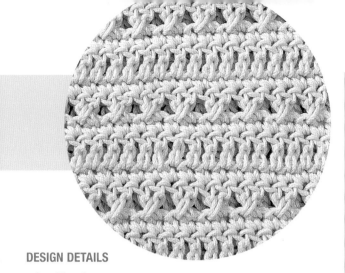

DESIGN DETAILS

- Semifitted
- Front neckline rests around collarbone
- Slight fullness gathered at waist with drawstring
- Shaped armhole
- Hood crocheted to neckline and seamed at top

FEATURED STITCHES

Chain (ch); see page 99

Double crochet (dc); see page 103

Double crochet 2 together (dc2tog); see page 112

Half double crochet (hdc); see page 103

Single crochet (sc); see page 100

Single crochet 2 together (sc2tog); see page 111

Slip stitch (sl st); see page 102

SIZING

To fit bust: 31½ (34¼, 37¼, 41, 43¼)"

Finished bust: 36 (39, 42, 46, 48)"

MATERIALS

10 (10, 10, 10, 12) skeins of Tahki *Cotton Classic* (100% cotton: 1¾ ozs./50 g; 108 yds./97 m); Natural

F/5 (4 mm) crochet hook

1 stitch marker

Three ⅜" buttons

GAUGE

16 sts and 10 rows to 4" in Cross Stitch pattern

CROSS STITCH PATTERN

NOTE: *The ch-3 turning chain counts as a stitch. In other words, work the last stitch of each row into the top of the turning chain of the previous row unless the instructions indicate otherwise. Don't work the first stitch of a row into the base of the turning chain unless told to make an*

increase. Also, place a marker on the right side to help you identify the outside of your finished work.

Multiple of 2 sts (add 1 st for base chain)

Foundation Row: Sc in 2nd ch from hook and in each ch across, turn.

Row 1 (WS): Ch 3 (count as dc), dc in next and each sc to end, turn.

Row 2 (RS): Ch 1, sc in first and each st to end, turn.

Row 3: Ch 3 (count as dc), sk first and next sc, dc in next sc, dc in closest skipped sc (work by wrapping hook as usual, placing hook behind dc just made, inserting hook into fabric from front to back, and completing st in usual manner), *sk next 2 sts, dc in next sc, dc in closest skipped st*, rep from * to * to last st, dc in last st, turn.

Row 4: As row 2.

Rep rows 1–4.

NOTE: *When the instructions call for increases and decreases in pattern rows, follow the instructions below. When working a row 3 after a dec row, the crossed double crochets may not align with the X shapes in previous rows. Don't try to maintain the established repeat.*

To Dec 1 St at Start of Row 1: Ch 3 (count as dc), dc2tog, cont as directed.

To Dec 1 St at End of Row 1: Work across to dec location, dc2tog, cont as directed.

To Dec 1 St at Start of Row 3: Ch 3 (count as dc), sk first and next st, dc2tog over next 2 sts, dc in closest skipped st, cont as directed.

To Dec 1 St at End of Row 3: Work in pat across to dec location (e.g. last 3 sts), dc2tog, cont as directed (e.g. dc in last st).

Back

Ch 73 (79, 85, 93, 97).

Row 1 (RS): Sc in 2nd ch from hook and in each ch to end, turn. [72 (78, 84, 92, 96) sts]

Starting with row 1 of Cross St pat, work even until 10" from beg, ending with WS row completed.

ARMHOLE SHAPING

Next Row (RS): Ch 1, sc in first and each st to last 3 sts, turn. Rem 3 sts unworked. [69 (75, 81, 89, 93) sts]

Next Row: Dec 1 st, work in pat as established across to last 5 sts, dc2tog, turn. Rem 3 sts unworked. [64 (70, 76, 84, 88) sts]

Work 4 more rows in pat as established, AT SAME TIME dec 1 st at beg and end of each row. [56 (62, 68, 76, 80) sts]

Cont in pat as established until 17 (17½, 18, 18, 18½)" from beg. Fasten off.

Front

Work as for back (including armhole shaping) until 12 (12½, 13, 13, 13½)" from beg, ending with WS row completed.

LEFT SHOULDER AND NECKLINE SHAPING

Next Row (RS): Sc in first 28 (32, 34, 38, 40) sts, turn. Rem sts unworked.

Work even in pat as established for 3", ending with pat row 3 completed.

Next Row (RS): Ch 1, sc in first 22 (26, 28, 32, 34) sts, turn. Rem 6 sts unworked.

Next Row: Sl st in first 4 sts, ch 3 (count as dc), dec 1 st, work in pat as established to end, turn. [18 (22, 24, 28, 30) sts]

Next Row: Ch 1, sc in first and each st across to last 2 sts, sc2tog, turn. [17 (21, 23, 27, 29) sts]

Next Row: Dc2tog, dc in next and each st to end, turn. [16 (20, 22, 26, 28) sts]

Cont in pat as established until 17 (17½, 18, 18, 18½)" from beg. Fasten off.

RIGHT SHOULDER AND NECKLINE SHAPING

Next Row: On last full row and with RS facing you, attach yarn with sc in next available center st, working toward unstitched shoulder, sc in all sts to end, turn. [28 (32, 34, 38, 40) sts]

Work even in pat as established for 3", ending with pat row 3 completed.

F O U N D A T I O N S
SHAPING—AND REVERSING SHAPING

Crocheted fabric is "shaped" when stitch changes alter its width and length. Usually, shaping helps a garment fit your body by increasing and decreasing stitches at one or both edges of the rows. You can also shape a garment by using shorter or taller stitches, as Tricia Crichton does in "Homespun Hug" (see page 45).

Sleeves for drop-shoulder sweaters, such as those in "Beginner's Luck" and "Fall Forward" (see pages 8 and 76) are good examples of basic shaping. As you build the sleeve fabric by stitching from wrist to shoulder, you're increasing stitches at both edges of the work. These increases widen the sleeve toward the top so that it will fit over your forearm, elbow, and upper arm.

"Reversing shaping" helps you create a second garment piece that's a mirror image of the one that you just made. The left and right fronts of "Summer Breeze" (see page 63) are good examples. Designer Nancy Brown starts by walking you through every stitch to make the left front of this garment. You follow these instructions to shape the armhole on the left edge of this piece and, a bit farther up, to make the decreases that shape the neckline on the right edge. The right front is a mirror image of the left front. Rather than providing full instructions for this second piece, Nancy tells you to follow the instructions for the left front, reversing the shaping as you stitch the upper rows. You stitch the shape in the same way you work the left front until you reach the armhole and neckline. At this point, you make increases and decreases on edges opposite to those specified for the left front, so that the armhole and neck will be positioned correctly on this piece. For example, you make increases at the ends of rows rather than at the beginning.

In *Crocheted Sweaters*, the term "reverse shaping" only appears in "Summer Breeze." In all the other sets of instructions that require reverse shaping, row-by-row instructions explain exactly what to do. In fact, if you've already made a sweater in this book, there's a good chance that you've done some reverse shaping! When you work the "Right Shoulder and Neckline Shaping" for the front of "Surf and Turf," for example, you're reversing the shaping.

Next Row (RS): Sl st in first 5 sts, sc2tog, sc in each st to end, turn. [22 (26, 28, 32, 34) sts]

Next Row (RS): Ch 3 (count as dc), dc in next and each st across to last 5 sts, dc2tog, turn. Rem 3 sts unworked. [18 (21, 24, 28, 30) sts]

Next Row: Ch 1, sc2tog first 2 sts, sc to end, turn. [17 (21, 23, 27, 29) sts]

Next Row: Ch 3 (count as dc), dc in next and each st across to last 2 sts, dc2tog, turn. [16 (20, 22, 26, 28) sts]

Cont in pat until 17 (17½, 18, 18, 18½)" from beg. Fasten off.

Hood

With RS tog, sew front to back at both shoulder seams. Starting at top of 3" opening, work 18 evenly spaced sc along right front neck, 40 sc across back neck, 18 sc along left front neck, turn. [76 sts]

Starting with pat row 1, work even for 14". Fasten off.

Finishing

Fold hood in half with RS tog and sew the top edge.

HOOD EDGING

With RS facing you and starting at bottom of 3" opening on right front neck, work 121 sc around entire hood, ending at bottom of 3" opening on left front, turn.

Next Row: Ch 1, sc in first st, *sk next sc, 4 hdc in next sc, sk next sc, sc in next sc*, rep from * to * to end. Fasten off.

Sew buttons to left side of center slash opening on front.

ARMHOLE EDGING

With RS facing you, work 65 evenly spaced sc along front and back armhole edge, turn.

Next Row: Ch 1, sc in first sc, *sk next sc, 4 hdc in next sc, sk next sc, sc in next sc*, rep from * to * to end. Fasten off.

Rep for other armhole. Sew side seams.

DRAWSTRING

Ch 146 (158, 170, 186, 194), turn.

Next Row: Ch 1, sc in 2nd ch from hook and each ch across. Fasten off.

Weave drawstring through every 2nd hole at the bottom of the sweater, starting and ending at center front.

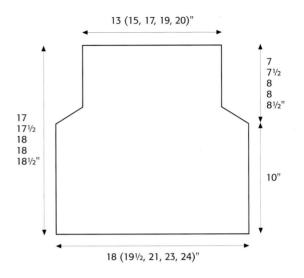

BACK

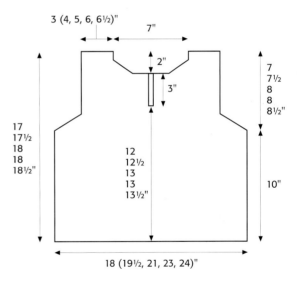

FRONT

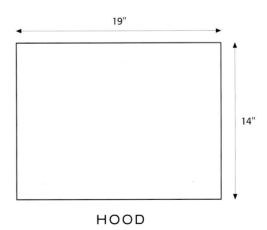

HOOD

Fall Forward

BY SUSAN HUXLEY

With its simple shaping and easy stitches, this stunning sweater makes an ideal project for beginning crocheters who'd like to learn how to increase and decrease. If you want to try working this garment in a different yarn, you'll find a wealth of solid and multicolored yarns available in the same weight as the one used here, in cottons, wools, and synthetics.

DESIGN DETAILS

- Crossed **X** (shown above) is stitched horizontally and seamed to armhole vertically
- Loose fitting
- Body length midway between high hip and full hip
- Drop shoulder, full-length sleeve
- Retro stand-up collar on wide neck opening

FEATURED STITCHES

Chain (ch); see page 99

Chain-space (ch-sp); see page 111

Double crochet (dc); see page 103

Single crochet (sc); see page 100

Slip stitch (sl st); see page 102

Treble crochet (tr); see page 104

SIZING

To fit bust: 31½ (34¼, 37¼, 41, 43¼)"

Finished bust: 37½ (40½, 42, 47, 49½)"

MATERIALS

9 (10, 10, 11, 12) hanks of Cascade *Pastaza* (50% llama, 50% wool: 3½ ozs./100 g; 132 yds./120 m); #1065 Ruby Heather

H/8 (5 mm) crochet hook

GAUGE

14 sts and 7 rows to 4" in dc

CROSSED X PATTERN

NOTE: *At the beginning of row 1, it may seem as if you're skipping 4 stitches. The turning chain acts as a treble stitch and ch-1 space. Remember that when the turning chain counts as a stitch, you don't work into the first stitch of the row (at the base of the turning chain); ignore the first "hole," skip 3 stitches, and make the first treble into the next stitch (the 4th stitch from the turning chain—or 5th if you include the hole at the base of the turning chain).*

Multiple of 4 sts + 3 (also add 1 st for base chain)

Foundation Row: Sc in 2nd ch from hook and in each st to end.

Row 1: Ch 5 (count as tr and ch-1 sp), sk next 3 sts, tr in next st, ch 1, tr in 2nd st to right of tr just made (work by wrapping hook as usual, placing hook behind tr just made, inserting hook into fabric from front to back, and completing st in usual manner), ch 1, *sk next 5 sts (including st with tr), tr in next st, ch 1, tr in 2nd st to right of tr just made, ch 1*, rep from * to * to last 2 sts, tr in last st, turn.

Rep row 1.

Back

Ch 64 (68, 72, 80, 84).

Row 1: Sc in 2nd ch from hook and in each st to end, turn. [63 (67, 71, 79, 83) sts]

Row 2: As Crossed X pat row 1.

Row 3: Ch 1, sc in first st, sc around next ch-sp, 2 sc in next and each ch-sp to tch, 2 sc around tch, turn. [63 (67, 71, 79, 83) sts]

Row 4: Ch 3 (count as dc), dc in next and each st to end, turn.

Rep row 4 until 12 (12, 12, 12, 12¼)" from beg.

ARMHOLE SHAPING

Next Row: Ch 1, sl st in first 7 (9, 9, 12, 13) sts, ch 3, dc in 50 (50, 54, 56, 58) sts, turn. Rem 6 (8, 8, 11, 12) sts unworked.

Next Row: As row 4.

Work even in dc rows until 9 (9½, 10, 10½, 11)" from beg of armhole shaping. Fasten off.

Front

Work as for back.

Sleeve (Make 2)

Ch 32 (33, 35, 35, 35).

Row 1: Dc in 4th ch from hook (count as 2 dc), dc in each ch to end, turn. [30 (31, 33, 33, 33) sts]

Row 2: Ch 3 (count as dc), dc in first st (base of tch), dc in next and each st across to last st, 2 dc in last st, turn. [32 (33, 35, 35, 35) sts]

Rep last row 0 (0, 0, 1, 1) more times. [32 (33, 35, 37, 37) sts]

Next Row: Ch 3 (count as dc), dc in first st (base of tch), dc in next and each st to end, turn. [33 (34, 36, 38, 38) sts]

Rep last row 26 (29, 31, 33, 33) more times. [59 (63, 67, 71, 71) sts]

Next Row: Ch 3 (count as dc), dc in next and each st to end, turn.

Cont working even in dc until 21¾ (22, 22½, 23, 23½)" from beg of sleeve.

Next Row: As row 2 of back.

Next Row: As row 3 of back. Fasten off.

Finishing

Block each garment piece.

With RS tog and edges matching, join front and back at right shoulder with a sl st in each of first 10 (10, 12, 13, 14) sts. Fasten off. Skip the center 31 stitches (neckline). Join the last 10 (10, 12, 13, 14) sts in the same manner.

Spread body out, RS up. Seam wide end of one sleeve, RS down, to long edge of one armhole. Then refold sweater to sew the 2 short sections of sleeve underarm edges to bottom edges of armhole. Attach rem sleeve to body in same manner. Block both seams.

Fold garment so RS is to inside, with sides of front and back matched. Also match underarms of folded sleeves.

Join front and back at one side with running-stitch seam from bottom edge to underarm. Without breaking yarn, continue stitching to close sleeve at underarm. Join other side of sweater in same manner.

Collar

Turn RS of sweater out, attach yarn at a shoulder seam.

Rnd 1: Ch 3 (count as dc), dc in next and each stitch to opposite shoulder seam, dc into shoulder seam, dc into each st around back neck, join to first st with sl st. [64 sts]

Rnd 2: Ch 3 (count as dc), dc in next and each stitch around, join with sl st.

Rnd 3: As rnd 2. Fasten off.

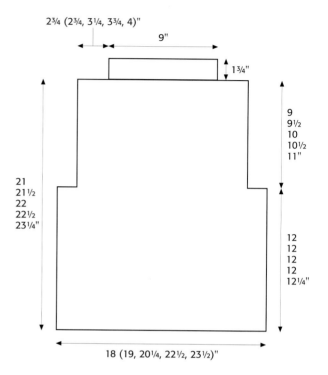

BACK/FRONT

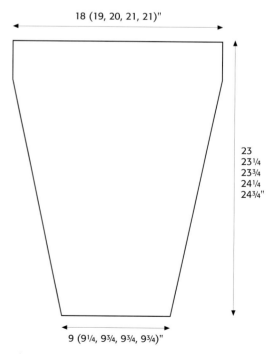

SLEEVE

Bright Idea

BY EDIE ECKMAN

*C*elebrate summer with this cheerful—and unabashedly colorful—short-sleeved
sweater. The lace-like pattern in the body, which consists of groups of treble crochet,
may be a bit challenging for beginners but really isn't as complex as it looks.

DESIGN DETAILS

- Semifitted
- Body length to below waist
- Modified drop shoulder; short, above-elbow sleeve

FEATURED STITCHES

Chain (ch); see page 99

Chain-space (ch-sp); see page 111

Double crochet (dc); see page 103

Single crochet (sc); see page 100

Slip stitch (sl st); see page 102

Treble crochet (tr); see page 104

SIZING

To fit bust: 31½ (34¼, 37¼, 41, 43¼)"

Finished bust: 37 (40, 43, 46, 49)"

MATERIALS

Lion Brand *MicroSpun* (100% microfiber acrylic: 2½ ozs./70 g; 168 yds./151 m): 7 (8, 9, 10, 11) balls of #148 Turquoise (MC); and 1 ball each of #186 Mango (A), #194 Lime (B), #146 Fuchsia (C), and #158 Buttercup (D)

F/5 (4 mm) crochet hook

GAUGE

20 sts and 18 rows to 4" in Granite Stitch pattern

SHELL TRELLIS PATTERN

Multiple of 5 sts (add 6 sts for base chain)

Foundation Row (WS): (Dc, ch 2, dc) in 8th ch from hook, *ch 3, sk 4 chs, (dc, ch 2, dc) in next ch*, rep from * to * to last 3 chs, ch 2, dc in last ch, turn.

Row 1: Ch 4 (count as tr), sk first ch-2 sp, 5 tr in next ch-2 sp, *sk ch-3 sp, 5 tr in next ch-2 sp*, rep from * to * to tch, sk 2 chs in tch, 1 tr in next ch, turn.

Row 2: Ch 5 (count as dc and ch-2 sp), *(dc, ch 2, dc) in middle tr of first 5-tr group, ch 3*, rep from * to * in each 5-tr group across to last st, ch 2, dc in last st (tch), turn.

Rep rows 1 and 2.

GRANITE STITCH PATTERN

NOTE: *Count the ch-1 turning chain as a stitch. In other words, work the last stitch of each row into the top of the turning chain of the previous row, unless the instructions indicate otherwise. Don't work the first stitch of a row into the base of the turning chain unless told to make an increase.*

Multiple of 2 sts

Foundation Row: Sc in 2nd ch from hook (count as sc), *ch 1, sk next ch, sc in next ch*, rep from * to *, turn.

Row 1: Ch 1 (count as st), sc in ch-1 sp, *ch 1, sk next sc, sc in next ch-1 sp*, rep from * to * to end, working last sc in top of tch, turn.

Rep row 1.

Back

With MC, ch 81 (86, 91, 96, 101).

Row 1 (WS): (Dc, ch 2, dc) in 8th ch from hook, *ch 3, sk 4 chs, (dc, ch 2, dc) in next ch*, rep from * to * to last 3 chs, ch 2, dc in last ch, turn. 108 (115, 122, 129, 136) sts]

Row 2: As Shell Trellis pat row 1. Cut MC, attach D. [77 (82, 87, 92, 97) sts]

Row 3: With D, as Shell Trellis pat row 2.

Row 4: With D, as Shell Trellis pat row 1. Cut D, attach C.

Rows 5 and 6: With C, rep rows 2 and 1. Cut C, attach B.

Rows 7 and 8: With B, rep rows 2 and 1. Cut B, attach A.

Rows 9 and 10: With A, rep rows 2 and 1. Cut A.

X-Small, Small, and Medium Only

Row 11: With MC, ch 1 (count as st), sc in next 1 (2, 0) tr, *sc in each of next 3 tr, 2 sc in next tr*, rep from * to * 16 (17, 20) more times, sc in each of next 6 (6, 1) tr, sc in top of tch, turn. [94 (100, 108) sts]

NOTE: *Instructions are continued on page 82.*

NOTE: *Instructions are continued on page 82.*

FOUNDATIONS

INTERNATIONAL SYMBOLS

Crocheters around the world share favorite instructions by using international symbols instead of row-by-row words and abbreviations.

As you can see below, crochet symbols are intuitive in design. A chain stitch, for example, is represented by an open oval, and the treble-crochet stitch—a stitch made by wrapping the yarn around the hook one more time than required for a double crochet—has one line more than the symbol for a double crochet. Some of the sweater instructions in this book tell you to work a stitch around a chain-space or between two stitches. This process is represented by placing a "hook" at the bottom of the stitch symbol.

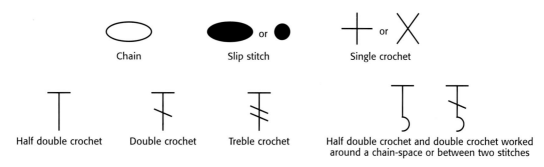

To "write" a set of instructions, the designer strings together the symbols to make a "row" of stitches. Even the turning chain is included. The rows are stacked to build the finished fabric.

Take a look at the chart below; it represents the instructions for the Granite Stitch pattern used in this sweater.

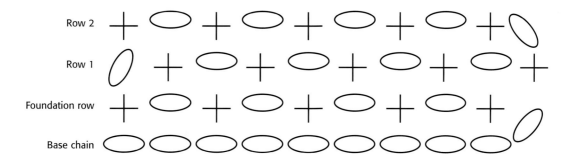

To follow these instructions, start by counting the number of ovals at the bottom of the chart. These represent the number of chains you work to make the base chain.

The end of the base chain curves up at the bottom right-hand corner of the chart. To the left of the curved section is the first stitch of the foundation row. Count the number of ovals in the curved area of the base chain. Then, on your base chain, count back the same number of chains from your hook, and place the first stitch of the foundation row in the next chain to the left. The skipped chain becomes the turning chain for the foundation row. In this example, only one chain is skipped, but the turning chain for a foundation row can consist of more than one stitch.

As you continue to crochet the foundation row into the base chain, follow the symbols from right to left. Turn your work at the end of the row. To make a turning chain for the new row, stitch the number of chains shown above the last stitch in the foundation row. Then stitch the next row by following the symbols in the second row above the base chain, this time reading from left to right. Continue stitching subsequent rows in this manner, changing direction at the end of every row.

Large Only

Row 11: With MC, ch 1 (count as st), sc in same sp, *sc in each of next 3 tr, 2 sc in next tr*, rep from * to * 22 times, sc in each of next 2 tr, 2 sc in top of tch, turn. [116 sts]

X-Large Only

Row 11: With MC, ch 1 (count as st), sc in same sp, sc in each of next 2 tr, *2 sc in next tr, sc in next 3 tr*, rep from * to * 22 more times, sc in next tr, 2 sc in top of tch, turn. [122 sts]

All Sizes

Row 12: Ch 1 (count as st), sc in next sc, *ch 1, sk 1 sc, sc in next sc*, rep from * to *, turn.

Work even in Granite St pat row 1 until 13½ (13¾, 14, 14¼, 14¼)" from beg.

ARMHOLE SHAPING

Next Row: Work in Granite St pat to last 6 (6, 8, 8, 10) sts, turn. [88 (94, 100, 108, 112) sts]

Rep last row 1 more time. [82 (88, 92, 100, 102) sts]

Work even in pat until 21 (22, 23, 23½, 24)" from beg, ending with RS row completed.

RIGHT SHOULDER SHAPING

Next Row (WS): Work in pat across 26 (28, 30, 32, 33) sts, turn. Rem 56 (60, 62, 68, 69) sts unworked.

Work even in pat for 1". Fasten off.

LEFT SHOULDER SHAPING

Next Row: With WS facing you, and working into same row as start of right shoulder shaping, sk 29 (31, 31, 35, 35) sts (for neckline), attach MC with sl st in next st. Work in Granite St pat across 26 (28, 30, 32, 33) sts, turn.

Work even in pat for 1". Fasten off.

Front

Work as for back to end of armhole shaping, until 17 (18, 19, 18½, 19)" from beg, ending with RS row completed.

LEFT SHOULDER SHAPING

Next Row (WS): Work in Granite St pat across 36 (38, 40, 44, 45) sts, turn. Rem 46 (50, 52, 56, 57) sts unworked.

Next Row: Work in pat to end, turn.

Next Row (Dec Row 1): Work in pat across 34 (36, 38, 42, 43) sts, sc in next st, turn. Rem 1 st unworked.

Next Row: Ch 2 (count as 1 st and ch-1 sp), sc in next ch-1 sp, work in pat to end, turn.

Next Row: Work in pat across 34 (36, 38, 42, 43) sts, turn. Rem 1 st unworked.

Next Row: Work in pat to end, turn.

Next Row: Work in pat across 32 (34, 36, 40, 41) sts, sc in next st, turn. Rem 1 st unworked.

Next Row: Ch 2 (count as 1 st and ch-1 sp), sc in next ch-1 sp, work in pat to end, turn.

Cont to dec in this manner until 26 (28, 30, 32, 33) sts. Work even in pat until same length as back. Fasten off.

RIGHT SHOULDER SHAPING

Next Row: With WS facing you, and working into same row as start of left shoulder shaping, sk 9 (11, 11, 11, 11) sts (for neckline), attach MC with sl st in next st, sc in next st, sc in ch-1 sp, *sk next sc, ch 1, sc in ch-1 sp*, rep from * to * across to tch, sc in tch, turn. [36 (38, 40, 44, 45) sts]

Starting with dec row 1 of left shoulder shaping, work right shoulder to match left. Fasten off.

Sleeve (Make 2)

With A, ch 56 (56, 61, 66, 70).

Rows 1 and 2: As rows 1 and 2 of back. Cut D. [52 (52, 57, 62, 66) sts]

Row 3 (WS): With MC, ch 1 (count as st), sc in each of next 0 (0, 0, 4, 6) tr, *sc in each of next 3 tr, 2 sc in next tr*, rep from * to * 11 (11, 12, 11, 12) more times, sc in each of next 2 (2, 3, 8, 6) tr, sc in tch, turn. [64 (64, 70, 74, 80) sts]

Row 4: Ch 1 (count as st), sc in next sc, *ch 1, sk 1 sc, sc in next sc*, rep from * to *, turn.

Row 5: Work in Granite St pat to end, turn.

Row 6: Ch 1 (count as st), sc in same st, sc in ch-1 sp, *ch 1, sk next sc, sc in ch-1 sp*, rep from * to * to last sc, sk last sc, ch-1, 2 sc in top of tch, turn. [66 (66, 72, 76, 82) sts]

Row 7: Ch 2 (count as sc and ch-1 sp), sc in ch-1, *ch 1, sk next sc, sc in ch-1 sp*, rep from * to * to last 2 sts, ch 1, sk 1 sc, sc in next sc, sc in top of tch, turn.

Row 8: Ch 1 (count as st), sc in first st, *ch 1, sk 1 sc, sc in ch-1 sp*, rep from * to * to tch, ch 1, sc in top of tch, turn. [68 (68, 74, 78, 84) sts]

Row 9: Work in Granite St pat to end, turn.

Cont in pat, inc every other row to 78 (88, 98, 100, 108) sts.

Work 2 rows even in pat.

Cont in pat, inc every 4th (4th, 4th, 4th, 0) row to 86 (92, 100, 102, 108) sts.

Work even in pat until 9½ (10, 10, 10, 10)" from beg. Fasten off.

Finishing

Block pieces. With RS tog, sew shoulder seams.

EDGING AND ASSEMBLY

With MC, sc evenly around neck, sk front and back corner stitches. Join with sl st to first st. Cut MC. Attach A. Ch 1, sc in each sc around. Fasten off.

With RS tog, sew front to back at side seams.

Fold a sleeve in half along its length, RS tog, aligning underarm edges. Sew these edges tog to make underarm seam. Turn sleeve RS out. Then slide sleeve into body until it's at an armhole. Align underarm and side seams, and match edge of sleeve with edge of armhole. Sew the edges together. Rep to make, insert, and join rem sleeve.

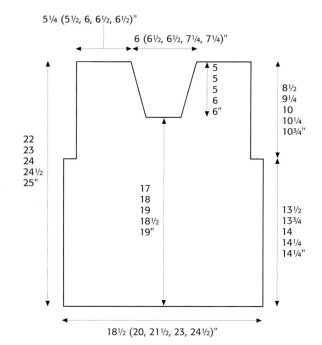

FRONT

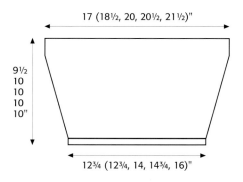

SLEEVE

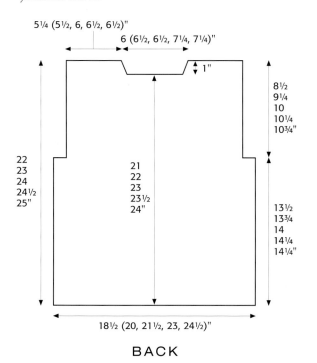

BACK

Lightning Strike

By SUSAN HUXLEY

Bolts of color zigzag down the front of this soft, cuddly sweater. The striking burgundy, black, and purple design is almost effortless because you use only one yarn—a spaced-dyed multicolor. (The length in the ball changes to a different color every twelve inches.) The stitching is simple and quick because the pattern is basic openwork that's made with a large hook.

DESIGN DETAILS

- Semifitted
- Body length between high and full hip
- Full-length sleeve worked from shoulder to wrist
- Slight drop shoulder

FEATURED STITCHES

Chain (ch); see page 99

Chain-space (ch-sp); see page 111

Half double crochet (hdc); see page 103

Slip stitch (sl st); see page 102

SIZING

To fit bust: 31½ (34¼, 37¼, 41, 43¼)"

Finished bust: 35 (38, 41, 45, 47)"

MATERIALS

11 (12, 13, 13, 14) balls of Filatura Cervinia *Geisha* (100% microfiber: 1¾ ozs./50 g; 76 yds./70 m); Color #1921 (MC)

1 ball of any smooth, medium-weight yarn, matched to one color in MC (A)

K/10.5 (7 mm) crochet hook

4 stitch markers

GAUGE

12 sts and 7 rows to 4" in Offset Filet pattern

OFFSET FILET PATTERN

NOTE: *Geisha is so fluffy that finding the stitches in a base chain is difficult, so make the length of chains with a smooth, medium-weight yarn (see "Materials").*

Multiple of 2 sts (add 1 st for base chain)

Base Chain: With A, chain desired number of sts. Fasten off.

Foundation Row: Join MC to last chain st with sl st. Ch 2 (count as hdc), hdc in next ch, *ch 1, sk 1 ch, hdc in next ch*, rep from * to * to end, turn.

Row 1: Ch 2 (count as hdc), *hdc around ch-sp, sk 1 hdc, ch 1*, rep from * to * across to last 2 hdc, sk 1 hdc, hdc around last hdc (tch), turn.

Rep row 1.

Back

With A, ch 54 (58, 62, 68, 72). Fasten off. Join MC to last ch.

Row 1: As foundation row of Offset Filet pat, turn. [54 (58, 62, 68, 72) sts]

Row 2: As Offset Filet pat row 1, turn.

Cont in pat until 21 (21½, 22, 22½, 23)" from beg. Fasten off.

Front

Work as for back until 20½ (21, 21½, 22, 22½)" from beg.

LEFT SHOULDER SHAPING

Next Row: Ch 2 (count as hdc), *hdc around ch-sp, sk 1 hdc, ch 1*, rep from * to * 5 (6, 7, 8, 9) more times, hdc around next ch-sp, turn. Rem 40 (42, 44, 48, 50) sts unworked.

Work 1 row even in pat. Fasten off.

RIGHT SHOULDER SHAPING

Next Row: Working on last full row, sk 25 (25, 25, 27, 27) sts in center (for neckline). Join yarn with sl st in next st (hdc). As pat row 1, turn. [14 (16, 18, 20, 22) sts]

Work 1 row even in pat. Fasten off.

Sleeve (Make 2)

With A, ch 46 (48, 52, 56, 60). Fasten off.

Row 1: As pat foundation row, turn. [46 (48, 52, 56, 60) sts]

Rep pat row 1 until 4 (4, 4, 0, 0)" from beg.

Next Row (Dec Row 1): Ch 3 (count as hdc and ch-sp), sk first ch-sp and hdc, hdc around next ch-sp, *sk 1 hdc, ch 1, hdc around next ch-sp*, rep from * to * across to last 2 sts (hdc and tch), sk 1 hdc, hdc around tch, turn. Place marker on last hdc of row just worked. [44 (46, 50, 54, 58) sts]

Next Row (Dec Row 2): Ch 2 (count as hdc), sk first ch-sp and hdc, *hdc around next ch-sp, sk 1 hdc, ch 1*, rep from * to * across to last st (tch, at marker), hdc around tch, turn. Move marker to last hdc of row just worked. [42 (44, 48, 52, 56) sts]

Work 3 rows even in pat.

Rep last 5 rows 4 (4, 5, 6, 7) more times. [26 (28, 28, 28, 28) sts]

Work even in pat until 21 (21, 21, 21, 21½)" from beg. Fasten off.

Collar

With RS tog, join front and back at right shoulder. (Left shoulder is not joined.) Along top edge of back, place marker 4¾ (5½, 5½, 6¾, 7¼)" from corner of left shoulder. Place marker on front in same manner.

Working on garment front, with RS facing you, join MC with sl st in ch-sp closest to marker.

Row 1: Ch 2 (count as hdc), sk next hdc, hdc around first ch-sp, *ch 1, sk 1 hdc, hdc around ch-sp*, rep from * to * across front and back neckline, ending in ch-sp closest to back marker, turn. Move marker on back to last hdc of row just worked.

Row 2: As dec row 1 of sleeve, turn. [2 st dec]

Row 3: As dec row 2 of sleeve, turn. [2 st dec]

Rep last 2 rows 5 more times. Fasten off. Remove markers.

Finishing

With RS tog, sew front and back at left shoulder. Don't join collar edges.

Spread joined, opened front and back flat on a table, with RS facing you. Place markers along each edge to mark armholes. Position sleeve across joined pieces, RS down, with wider end between markers on one side and aligned with edge of armhole. Sew sleeve to body. Attach rem sleeve in the same manner.

Remove markers. Refold body and sleeves, RS tog, aligning all matching edges. Join front to back by sewing up sides and along sleeve underarms.

EDGING

To hide the base chain made with A, join MC in ch-sp near side seam at bottom of body.

Rnd 1: *Sc around both loops of A in base of next hdc, sc around next ch-sp*, rep from * to * around bottom of sweater, join to first st with sl st. Fasten off.

Stitch around bottoms of sleeves in same manner.

F O U N D A T I O N S
FILET CROCHET

Usually worked in a series of double crochet "bars" linked by two chain stitches, filet crochet creates a gridded fabric. Lovely free-flowing motifs, geometric designs, and words are built into the work by filling select holes in the grid with more double crochet as each row is made. The stitching is simple until you tackle advanced work, such as turning corners and edging the finished pieces.

Traditionally, filet crochet is worked with crochet cotton, and the fabric is used to make tablecloths, curtains, and linens, but filet crochet can also be used to create wonderful beach cover-ups and other garments. The sweater featured here pushes the traditional boundaries even further. It's worked in half double crochet, which is less "twisty" than double crochet, and there's only one single crochet between the vertical bars. This offset filet is perfect for fancy yarn that needs room to fluff out. You don't have to struggle to find the stitches in the previous row because the new row is worked into the obvious horizontal bars created by the chain stitches between the half double crochets.

4¾ (5½, 5½, 6¾, 7¼)"

8 (8½, 9, 9¼, 9½)"

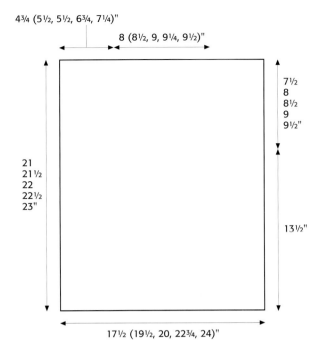

7½
8
8½
9
9½"

13½"

21
21½
22
22½
23"

17½ (19½, 20, 22¾, 24)"

BACK

15 (16, 17, 18, 19)"

21
21
21
21
21½"

8¼ (9¼, 9¼, 9¼, 9¼)"

SLEEVE

4¾ (5½, 5½, 6¾, 7¼)"

8 (8½, 9, 9¼, 9½)"

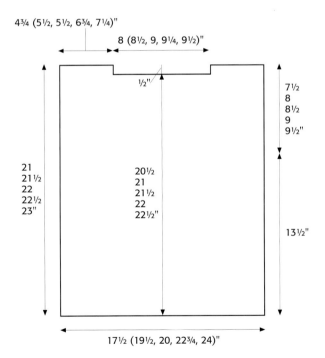

½"

7½
8
8½
9
9½"

13½"

21
21½
22
22½
23"

20½
21
21½
22
22½"

17½ (19½, 20, 22¾, 24)"

FRONT

Loopy Idea

BY NANCY NEHRING

A sparkly yarn and fashion-forward cuffs and collar make the ordinary extraordinary. Even though this sweater is fitted, you don't have to fuss with counting rows and stitches because the finished garment stretches for a custom fit.

DESIGN DETAILS

• Close fitting
• Body length to high hip
• Full length, set-in sleeve
• Short garment pieces lengthen as worn
• Shoulder seam stabilized with ribbon or twill tape

FEATURED STITCHES

Chain (ch); see page 99

Chain-space (ch-sp); see page 111

Half double crochet (hdc); see page 103

Half double crochet 2 tog (hdc2tog); see page 112

Loop stitch variation (lsv); see page 105

Single crochet (sc); see page 100

Slip stitch (sl st); see page 102

SIZING

To fit bust: 31½ (34¼, 37¼, 41, 43¼)"

NOTE: *The loop stitch is heavy, while the yarn and half double crochet (ground) stitch stretch slightly. The first time that you wear the finished sweater, it will lengthen for a closer fit than implied by the measurements of the garment pieces. Work the garment size that matches your body size, as listed in "To fit bust."*

MATERIALS

9 (10, 11, 12, 13) skeins of Skacel *Charming* (40% cotton, 25% acrylic, 17% metallic, 10% polyester, 8% nylon: 1¾ ozs./50 g; 104 yds./94 m); Color #01

G/6 (4.25 mm) hook

Six ½"-wide rhinestone buttons

12" of ¼"-wide ribbon or twill tape

Sharp sewing needle

Sewing thread, color-matched to yarn

GAUGE

NOTE: *The yarn and stitch have built-in stretch; just lifting the gauge swatch makes it longer. Place the swatch loosely on a flat surface. Gently stroke the swatch vertically to flatten it before measuring.*

12 sts and 11 rows to 4" in hdc

LOOP EDGING PATTERN

NOTE: *Don't count the ch-1 turning chain at the start of the row as a stitch. Work the next stitch of the new row into the first stitch of the previous row. At the end of the row, don't work into the turning chain of the previous row.* NOTE ALSO: *A ch-2 turning chain (as in row 9) does count as a stitch. In other words, make the following stitch into the next stitch of the previous row, and work the last stitch of the new row into the top of the turning chain of the previous row, unless the instructions indicate otherwise.*

Worked over any number of sts (add 1 st for base chain)

Row 1 (RS): Sc in 2nd ch from hook and in each st across, turn.

Rows 2, 4, 6, and 8: Ch 1, lsv in first and each st to last st, sl st in last st, turn.

Rows 3, 5, and 7: Ch 1, *sc in first st, sk next st*, rep from * to * to last st, sc in last st, turn.

Row 9: Ch 2 (count as hdc), hdc in next and every other st to end, turn.

Rep rows 2–9.

Left Front

Ch 23 (25, 27, 30, 32).

Row 1 (RS): Sc in 2nd ch from hook and in each st to end, turn. [22 (24, 26, 29, 31) sc]

Row 2: As Loop Edging pat row 2.

Cont in pat as established until row 9 completed.

Row 10: Ch 2 (count as hdc), hdc in next and each st to end, turn.

Rep last row 16 more times, AT SAME TIME work 2 hdc in last st of row 12, then every 4th row. [26 (28, 30, 33, 35) hdc]

ARMHOLE SHAPING

Row 27: Sl st in first 2 (3, 4, 4, 6) sts, ch 2 (count as hdc), hdc2tog, hdc in next and each st to end, turn. [24 (25, 26, 29, 29) sts]

Row 28: Ch 2 (count as hdc), hdc across to last 3 sts, hdc2tog, turn. Rem st unworked. [22 (23, 24, 27, 27) sts]

Row 29: Ch 2 (count as hdc), sk next st, hdc2tog, hdc to end, turn. [20 (21, 22, 25, 25) sts]

Work even in hdc for 8 (10, 10, 12, 12) rows.

NECKLINE SHAPING

Next Row: Sl st in first 1 (1, 2, 3, 3) st(s), sc in next st, hdc to end, turn. [19 (20, 20, 22, 22) sts]

Next Row: Ch 2 (count as hdc), 2 hdc in next st, hdc in next and each st across to last 3 sts, hdc2tog, turn. Rem st unworked. [18 (19, 19, 21, 21) sts]

Next Row: Ch 2 (count as hdc), hdc2tog, hdc in next and each st to end, turn. [17 (18, 18, 20, 20) sts]

Next Row: Ch 2 (count as hdc), 2 hdc in next st, hdc in next and each st across to last 3 sts, hdc2tog, turn. Rem st unworked. [16 (17, 17, 19, 19) sts]

Next Row: Ch 2 (count as hdc), hdc2tog, hdc to end, turn. [15 (16, 16, 18, 18) sts]

SHOULDER SHAPING

Next Row: Sl st in first st, sc in each of next 2 sts, ch 1, hdc in first and each hdc across to last 2 sts, hdc2tog, turn. [13 (14, 14, 16, 16) sts]

Next Row: Ch 2 (count as hdc), hdc2tog, hdc in next and each st across to last 3 sts, sc in next st, turn. Rem 2 sts unworked. [10 (11, 11, 13, 13) sts]

Next Row: Sl st in each of first 3 sts, sc in next hdc, hdc in next and each st to end, turn. [7 (8, 8, 10, 10) sts]

Next Row: Ch 2 (count as hdc), hdc in next and each hdc across to last 3 sts, hdc2tog, turn. Rem st unworked. [5 (6, 6, 8, 8) sts]

Next Row: Ch 2 (count as hdc), hdc2tog, hdc in next and each hdc to end. Fasten off. [4 (5, 5, 7, 7) sts]

Loops must be set to prevent unraveling. Tug each one so that the sl st around the base of each loop forms a tight knot.

Right Front

Work as for left front to end of row 10.

Rep last row 16 more times, AT SAME TIME work 2 hdc in first st of Row 12, then every 4th row. [26 (28, 30, 33, 35) sts]

ARMHOLE SHAPING

Row 27: Ch 2 (count as hdc), hdc in next and each st across to last 3 (4, 5, 5, 7) sts, hdc2tog, turn. Rem 1 (2, 3, 3, 5) st(s) unworked.

Row 28: Ch 2 (count as hdc), sk next st, hdc2tog, hdc in next and each st to end, turn. [22 (23, 24, 27, 27) sts]

Row 29: Ch 2 (count as hdc), hdc in next and each st across to last 3 sts, hdc2tog, turn. Rem st unworked. [20 (21, 22, 25, 25) sts]

Work even in hdc for 8 (10, 10, 12, 12) rows.

NECKLINE SHAPING

Next Row: Ch 2 (count as hdc), hdc in next and each st across to last 2 (2, 3, 4, 4) sts, hdc2tog, turn. Rem 0 (0, 1, 2, 2) st(s) unworked.

Next Row: Ch 2 (count as hdc), sk 1 st, hdc2tog, hdc in next and each st across to last st, 2 hdc in last st, turn. [18 (19, 19, 21, 21) sts]

Next Row: Ch 2 (count as hdc), hdc in next and each st across to last 2 sts, hdc2tog, turn. [17 (18, 18, 20, 20) sts]

Next Row: Sl st in first 2 sts, ch 2 (count as hdc), hdc2tog, hdc in next and each st across to last st, 2 hdc in last st, turn. [16 (17, 17, 19, 19) sts]

Next Row: Ch 2 (count as hdc), hdc in next and each st across to last 2 sts, hdc2tog, turn. [15 (16, 16, 18, 18) sts]

SHOULDER SHAPING

Next Row: Ch 2 (count as hdc), hdc2tog, hdc in next and each st across to last 3 sts, hdc2tog, turn. Rem st unworked. [12 (13, 13, 15, 15) sts]

Next Row: Sl st in first st, sc in next st, hdc in next and each st across to last 2 sts, hdc2tog, turn. [10 (11, 11, 13, 13) sts]

Next Row: Ch 2 (count as hdc), hdc2tog, hdc in next and each st across to last 3 sts, sc in next st, turn. Rem 2 sts unworked. [7 (8, 8, 10, 10) sts]

Next Row: Sl st in first st, hdc2tog, hdc in next and each st to end, turn. [5 (6, 6, 8, 8) sts]

Next Row: Ch 2 (count as hdc), hdc in next and each st across to last 2 sts, hdc2tog. Fasten off. [4 (5, 5, 7, 7) sts]

Set loop stitches.

Back

Ch 45 (49, 53, 59, 63).

Row 1 (RS): Sc in 2nd st from hook and in each st to end, turn. [44 (48, 52, 58, 62) sts]

Row 2: Work across in Loop Edging pat row 2.

Cont in pat as established until Loop Edging pat row 9 completed.

Row 10: Ch 2 (count as hdc), hdc in next and each st across, turn.

Rep last row 16 more times, AT SAME TIME work 2 hdc in first and last st of row 12, then every 4th row. [52 (56, 60, 66, 70) sts]

ARMHOLE SHAPING

Row 27: Sl st in first 2 (3, 4, 4, 6) sts, ch 2 (count as hdc), hdc2tog, hdc in next and each st across to last 3 (4, 5, 5, 7) sts, hdc2tog, turn. Rem 1 (2, 3, 3, 5) st(s) unworked. [48 (50, 52, 58, 58) sts]

Row 28: Ch 2 (count as hdc), hdc2tog, hdc in next and each st across to last 2 sts, hdc2tog, turn. [46 (48, 50, 56, 56) sts]

Rep last row 3 more times. [40 (42, 44, 50, 50) sts]

Work even in hdc for 8 (10, 10, 12, 12) rows.

Next Row: Ch 2 (count as hdc), 2 hdc in next st, hdc in next and each st across to last st, 2 hdc in next st, turn. [42 (44, 46, 52, 52) sts]

Work 1 row even in hdc.

Next Row: Ch 2 (count as hdc), 2 hdc in next st, hdc in next and each st across to last st, 2 hdc in last st, turn. [44 (46, 48, 54, 54) sts]

Next Row: Sl st in next 2 sts, sc in next st, hdc across to last 3 sts, hdc2tog, turn. Rem st unworked. [40 (42, 44, 50, 50) sts]

LEFT SHOULDER SHAPING

Next Row (Dec Row 1): Sl st in next 2 sts, sc in next st, hdc in next 8 (9, 9, 11, 11) hdc, hdc2tog, turn. Rem 27 (28, 30, 34, 34) sts unworked.

Next Row (Dec Row 2): Ch 2 (count as hdc), hdc2tog, hdc in next and each st across to last 4 sts, hdc2tog, turn. Rem 2 sts unworked. [6 (7, 7, 9, 9) sts]

Next Row (Dec Row 3): Ch 2 (count as hdc), hdc in next and each st to end, turn. [5 (6, 6, 8, 8) sts]

Next Row (Dec Row 4): Ch 2 (count as hdc), hdc in next and each st across to last 2 sts, hdc2tog. Fasten off. Set loop stitches. [4 (5, 5, 7, 7) sts]

RIGHT SHOULDER SHAPING

Next Row (RS): With RS facing you and working into last full-length row, attach yarn with sc in top of 3rd hdc from right corner, hdc in first 7 (8, 8, 10, 10) sts, hdc2tog, turn. [10 (11, 11, 13, 13) sts]

Next 3 Rows: As back left shoulder dec rows 2, 3, and 4. [4 (5, 5, 7, 7) sts]

Sleeve (Make 2)

Ch 27 (29, 31, 35, 36).

Work as for left front to end of row 10. [27 (29, 31, 35, 36) sts]

Rep last row 26 more times, AT SAME TIME work 2 hdc in last st of row 12, then every 5th row 4 times, then every 3rd row once. [33 (35, 37, 41, 42) sts]

Row 37: Sl st in first 2 (3, 3, 3, 3) sts, ch 2 (count as hdc), hdc in next and each st across to last 3 sts, turn. Rem sts unworked. [28 (29, 31, 35, 36) sts]

Row 38: Ch 2 (count as hdc), hdc2tog, hdc in next and each st across to last 2 sts, hdc2tog, turn. [26 (27, 29, 33, 34) sts]

Rep last row 3 more times. [20 (21, 23, 27, 28) sts]

Work 2 (4, 4, 6, 6) rows even in hdc.

Rep row 38 five more times. [10 (11, 13, 17, 18) sts]

Next Row: Sl st in first 2 sts, ch 2 (count as hdc), hdc in next and each st across to last 2 sts, hdc2tog, turn. [6 (7, 9, 13, 14) sts]

Rep last row 1 more time. Fasten off. [2 (3, 5, 9, 10) sts]

Set loop stitches.

Finishing

With RS tog, sew fronts to back at shoulder and side seams.

Fold a sleeve in half along its length, RS tog, aligning underarm edges. Sew these edges tog to make underarm seam. Turn sleeve RS out. Then slide sleeve into body until it's at an armhole. Align underarm and side seams, and match edge of sleeve with edge of armhole. Sew the edges together. Rep to make, insert, and join rem sleeve.

Neckband

Row 1 (RS): Attach yarn at front of neck. Work 2 sc in side of each hdc along front and over shoulder, 1 sc in each hdc across back, 2 sc in side of each hdc over rem shoulder and front neck, turn.

Rows 2, 4, and 6 (WS): Ch 1, sk first st, work across in Loop Edging pat to last st, sk last st, turn.

Rows 3, 5, and 7: Ch 1, sk first 2 sl sts, *sc in every other st to just before shoulder seam, sk 2 sts, sc in shoulder seam, sk 2 sts*, rep from * to * once, sc in every other st to last 2 sts, turn. Rem 2 sts unworked. Fasten off. Set loop stitches.

Left Front Band

Row 1 (RS): Attach yarn at neckline. Working tightly, make 6 sc in end sts of neckband, sc in each of first 2 hdc along front edge of neckband, 2 sc in next st, sc in each of next 2 sts, sc along vertical edge of front to start of loops, make 9 more sc to end of loop edging, turn. [56 (58, 58, 60, 62) sts]

F O U N D A T I O N S
ADAPTING A PATTERN

If you've made more than one sweater, there's a good chance that you've already adapted a pattern. Perhaps you changed the sleeve length, chose buttons that were different from those recommended, or even used another yarn. Kudos for exercising your creativity!

Every sweater in this book is accompanied by a detailed list of materials that you need to make the featured garment, and by explicit instructions to guide you through the creation process. But, just in case you need it, you have permission to change anything that strikes your fancy.

Following are a few more ways to turn your sweater into a one-of-a-kind garment:

Button up. Anyone who has ever visited a well-stocked button shop can testify that switching buttons is one of the simplest and most dramatic ways to change a sweater's look—and certainly one that's lots of fun.

Add beads or trim. Forget tedious hours of hand sewing! At fabric and craft shops, you can buy beads, fringe, and other wonderful tidbits that are already attached to narrow fabric strips. Just use a simple running stitch to sew the strip to the bottom of the sweater. Hide the fabric strip on the wrong side, with the beads hanging below the crocheted edge or, if the fabric strip is decorative, sew it to the outside.

Stitch a new edging. Crocheters are so fascinated with edgings that entire books are dedicated exclusively to suitable stitches and patterns. When adding an edging to a sweater, just make sure that that the first round or row of the new edging has approximately the same number of stitches as the edging recommended in the pattern.

Add pompoms. Who says an edging has to be flat—or boring? Fashion designers have been adding little pompoms to sweater hems for many years. The look is fun and funky.

Color your world. You don't have to make a sweater in the same colors shown in the photo. At a yarn shop, hold several colors of the recommended yarn up to your face, one at a time, while you look in a mirror. Choose the color that's the most flattering. Yes, you want people to admire your finished sweater, but you also want them to notice that you look great in it!

Create stripes. A sweater may be shown in only one color, but yours doesn't have to look the same. Try changing the yarn color every few rows or inches. Make the switch at the edge by using the new yarn to stitch the turning chain for the new row. And your stripes don't have to be in different colors. As long as the yarn gauge is the same and the featured stitch is suitable, you can use yarns of varying textures to make the stripes.

Rows 2–7: Ch 1, sc in first and each st to end, turn.

Row 8: Ch 1, sc in first and each st to end. Fasten off.

Right Front Band

Attach yarn at neckline.

Rows 1 and 2: As for left front band.

Rep last row (row 2) two more times.

Row 5 (Buttonholes): Ch 1, 3 (4, 4, 5, 6) sc, ch 1, sk 1
(ch-1 sp made), *9 sc, ch 1, sk 1*, rep from * to * 4
more times, 2 (3, 3, 4, 5) sc, turn.

Rep row 2 two more times, working 1 sc around each
ch-1 sp.

Row 8: Sc across. Fasten off.

Tape Shoulder Seams

All of the sweater's weight hangs from the shoulders.
Since the crocheted fabric is stretchy, the shoulders
will distort unless they're reinforced. Cut 2 lengths of
¼"-wide ribbon or twill tape, each piece 1" longer
than the shoulder seam. On the WS, lay 1 length over
each shoulder seam. Turn under ½" at each end of
both lengths. With a sharp needle and sewing thread,
sew all edges of the lengths over the shoulder seams.
Shake edges of cardigan to fluff loops.

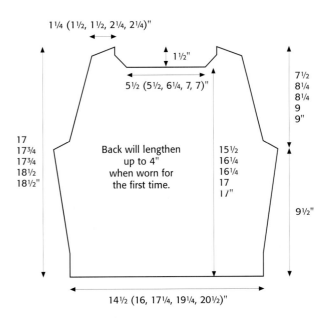

BACK

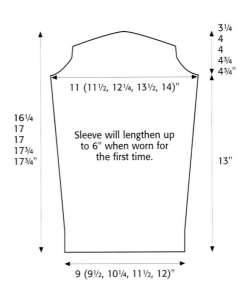

SLEEVE

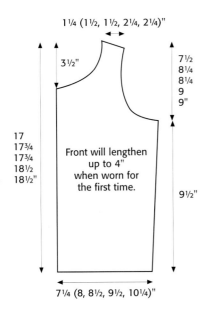

FRONT

All About Crochet

"*R*ight over left, and under; left over right, and under." Sound familiar? Learning to tie your shoelaces was a challenge, wasn't it? And an important rite of passage. Now, though, the process seems so simple. With a bit of practice and a little patience, you'll soon feel the same way about crocheting.

Don't let the thought of making the sweaters in this book intimidate you. Crocheting is just the simple process of making knots in yarn by using a stick with a hook on one end. "All About Crochet" will teach you everything you need to know. You'll be introduced to the supplies you need, walked through the process of crocheting your first piece of fabric, and guided—step-by-step—through making every stitch used in the featured sweaters. You'll also find help interpreting and following crochet instructions, tips on perfecting the fit of your sweater, and more.

Many lifelong stitchers, myself included, learned to crochet just a few years after we started tying our shoelaces. With this book in hand, you'll soon be tying bows—and filling your wardrobe with a glorious array of crocheted sweaters.

Nifty Notions and Yarns

Although I've been crocheting for decades, most of the items I use for my crochet work still fit into a single dresser drawer. You need so little to create wonderful garments! My yarn stash, however, is another matter. Like the collection of any avid stitcher, mine fills a walk-in closet—and then some. (Whoever dies with the most yarn wins!)

Crochet hooks come in a variety of sizes. When I was nine years old, my grandmother gave me a complete set of hooks that I use to this day. Consider buying a full set for yourself so you won't have to run to the store whenever you need a different one.

Depending on the manufacturer, hooks are sized in three different ways: U.S., metric, and U.K. The instructions in this book specify which U.S. or metric size to use, and the chart on page 126 provides equivalent sizes for all three systems. You may need to go up or down a size depending on how tightly or loosely you work your stitches (see "Gauge" on page 115).

I prefer a hook with a handle that has a flat spot on it so the hook doesn't spin in my hand, but another handle shape, from Skacel Collection, Inc. (see "Acknowledgments and Resources" on page 127), has recently caught my attention. The Skacel handle is round, comfortable to hold, and grooved to prevent spinning.

Large needles are necessary for weaving in loose yarn ends and for seaming the pieces of a sweater with a running stitch. Use a blunt needle, which won't split the yarn strands in the fabric, for weaving in loose ends, and a sharp-pointed needle for seaming. A good crochet tool kit has two tapestry needles in it, one with a sharp tip and one with a blunt tip.

Needle cases are great for storing and transporting needles. A magnetic version prevents the needles from popping out when you open the lid.

Small scissors—sharp and pointed—are best for snipping yarn.

Stitch markers, which are available at yarn shops, are small split rings, triangles, or squares that clip onto your work to help you count rows and track shaping, identify the right side of the work, and record pattern repeats.

Safety pins are the duct tape of the stitching world. You can use them to pin garment pieces together in order to check fit before permanently seaming the pieces, and they make wonderful substitutes when gremlins run off with your stitch markers.

A tension gauge measure—a flat, plastic frame with a 4"-square opening in its center—is handy for measuring the gauge (or tension) of your crocheted stitches. (See "Gauge" on pages 115–116 for more information.) You can use a ruler instead or make your own tension gauge measure from a sheet of quilting template material.

An iron with a burst-of-steam feature is a luxury worth owning. Blocking (using moisture to set the shapes of crocheted garment pieces) is especially easy when you can control the amount and timing of the shots of steam you apply. For more information on blocking, see page 119.

Towels are useful when you want to block garments without steaming them.

Rustproof T-pins—available at yarn, craft, and art-supply shops—hold sweater pieces in place while you block them. The pins must be able to withstand moisture (and heat, if you block with steam) without transferring rust deposits to your fabric. Some designers prefer plastic T-pins, but I haven't found any strong enough to puncture the corkboard that I use as a blocking surface.

Corkboard, thick cardboard, or a wide, heavily padded ironing board will work well as a blocking surface. The surface must be heat resistant and porous in order to help the crocheted fabric dry, and sufficiently strong to hold the T-pins in place. I use a cork bulletin board. It's large enough to hold a tunic-length sweater front, thick enough to protect the surface underneath it from moisture, and sturdy enough not to buckle when I lift and move it with the pinned, drying sweater piece on top.

A tape measure and ruler are both necessary for taking critical measurements. You may also want to purchase a T-square or triangle to help you square garment shapes before blocking them.

Yarns come in balls or loosely wound, folded oval skeins or hanks. If you've already discovered a fantastic array in your local yarn shop, you probably know how addictive selecting and purchasing yarn can be!

Newcomers to crochet will find it easiest to work with smooth yarns that aren't too slippery, stretchy, or fuzzy, but the yarns you choose don't have to be boring. Go for that gorgeous hand-painted yarn. Choose an alpaca and wool blend. Wrap yourself up in luxury.

To help you avoid frustration and disappointment, many of the sweaters in this book are made with simple yarns. You won't have to sell your car to buy them, the strands won't stick together if you have to rip apart a few rows, and stitching with them is easy. A couple of sweaters feature slightly challenging novelty yarns, but they're introduced in easy patterns. As your skills increase, so will the repertoire of yarns you can comfortably use.

If you'd like to use a yarn that's caught your fancy rather than one that's specified in the sweater instructions, turn to "A Visual Guide to Featured Yarns" on pages 124–125. In that section, you'll find photographs of the yarns used in this book and information that will help you find suitable substitutes. The wrapper around a ball, skein, or hank usually includes the manufacturer's name, the yarn's name, the fiber composition, the weight of the unit, the length, and the gauge of a swatch worked with a recommended knitting-needle size. If you're lucky, the wrapper may also provide the crochet gauge and recommended hook size.

Crocheting Your First Swatch

The brief tutorial that follows is a guided tour through the basics of crocheting—a lesson designed to walk the beginning crocheter through making a first swatch of fabric. You can use any size yarn and hook during this practice session, but a smooth, medium-weight yarn will be easiest to handle. The staff at your local yarn shop can recommend a hook size for the yarn you select.

Holding a Crochet Hook

There are two common ways to hold a crochet hook. Both may feel awkward at first. If neither is comfortable after you've practiced, just improvise. You can hold a hook any way you like, as long as you can control the yarn tension by feeding the yarn strand evenly to the hook.

I hold my hook in almost the same way as a child grasps a fork, with the base of the hook in my fist, my forefinger extended along the top, and my thumb opposite to my forefinger (see fig. 1). The grip of my pinkie and the finger next to it is relaxed.

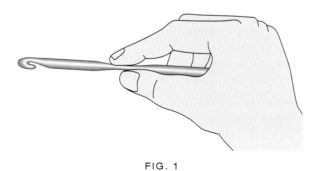

FIG. 1

You can also hold the hook by grasping it as if it were a pencil, with the end of the hook extending from the nook between your forefinger and thumb (see fig. 2).

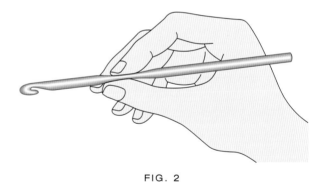

FIG. 2

Tying a Slip Knot

Before you start making stitches, you must secure a yarn loop on your hook. Start by making a loop near the end of the yarn and placing it on top of the yarn that's feeding from the ball or skein (see fig. 3).

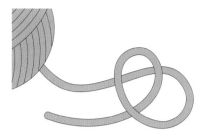

FIG. 3

Reach into the loop, grasp the strand inside it, and pull the strand through the loop (see fig. 4).

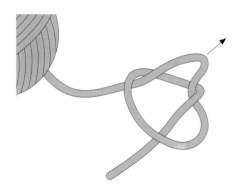

FIG. 4

Place the loop on the crochet hook. Pull on the yarn until the knot tightens on the hook (see fig. 5), but make sure the knot is loose enough to slide easily up and down the hook.

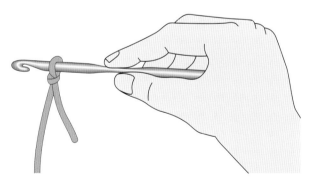

FIG. 5

Making a Base Chain

The chain is the most versatile stitch in any crocheter's repertoire. In fact, most crochet work starts with a length of these stitches, which is called the "base chain." You'll also use chains to help you turn your work at the start or end of a row (see "Turning Chains" on pages 108–109), and many patterns include this humble stitch.

To start the first chain stitch, wrap the yarn over the hook from right to left (see fig. 6). This process, known as "yarn over," is abbreviated as "YO."

Holding the yarn slightly taut with your left hand, pull the hook and wrapped yarn through the slip knot until the knot comes off the hook. To maintain tension on the yarn strand, I feed it to the hook through the fingers of my left hand, as shown.

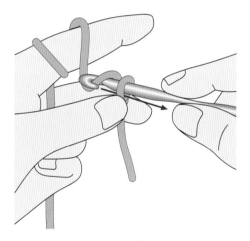

FIG. 6

Complete the base chain by making five more chain stitches (see fig. 7).

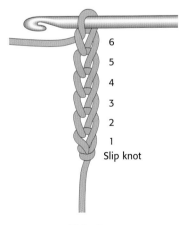

6
5
4
3
2
1
Slip knot

FIG. 7

Crocheting the First Row

In this swatch, row 1 consists of single-crochet stitches— short little knots that you can use to make an entire sweater or combine with other stitches in a pattern.

To begin the first single-crochet stitch in this row, insert the hook, from front to back, into the top loop of the second stitch from the hook so that there are two loops on the hook. Why the second stitch and not the first? As you complete this first stitch, the chain that you skipped will pull up vertically and will serve to keep the edge of the swatch straight. This "turning chain" also raises your hook to the level of the single-crochet stitches in the row you're about to create. (To learn more about turning chains, see pages 108–109.)

YO, and pull the loop through the chain-stitch loop (see fig. 8). One tip here: Each chain stitch is made up of three strands of yarn. Some crocheters pick up the back loop instead of the top loop; others pick up both loops. The best method for beginners—and the one you should use as you make the sweaters in this book—is to pick up the top loop only. You may choose any of these methods as you make garments that aren't in this book, but once you've made your choice, be consistent.

FIG. 8

Now YO again, and pull the yarn through both loops on the hook (see figs. 9 and 10). You've just made your first single crochet.

FIG. 9

FIG. 10

To make the next single crochet in row 1, insert the hook, from front to back, into the top loop of the next stitch (don't skip a chain this time). YO, pull the loop through the stitch, YO again, and pull the yarn through both loops on the hook.

Complete row 1 by making a single-crochet stitch in each of the three remaining chain stitches. Be careful not to make a stitch in the slip knot. Row 1 now has five single-crochet stitches; you don't count the turning chain you made as a stitch.

Now turn the crocheted fabric so the opposite side faces you. Remember which way you turned the work; you must turn it in the same direction for every row.

Making a Turning Chain

Every time you start a new row, you must "lift" your hook to the height of the first stitch that you're going to make in that row. You do this by making a turning chain, which consists of one or more chain stitches, depending on how tall the first stitch in the new row will be. The turning chain for a single crochet, which is a very short stitch, is just one chain. (See "Turning Chains" on pages 108–109.) Make that chain stitch now.

Stitching More Rows

As you create each subsequent row, you'll work your stitches into the top of the previous row. Before you start, look closely at the single-crochet stitches in row 1. You'll see that each stitch is topped with two loops. Be sure to pick up *both* loops each time you insert your hook into a stitch.

Now start row 2 by making a single-crochet stitch in the first stitch at the end of the previous row. In other words, ignore the chain that you just made, and work your first single crochet into the two side-by-side loops that are next to the hook. You're working into the stitch that the turning chain is built on.

Make four more single-crochet stitches, one into each stitch of the previous row. Turn the work in the same direction that you flipped it the first time; this direction must be consistent for every row.

Start row 3 as you did row 2 by making one chain stitch to serve as a turning chain. Then make a single-crochet stitch in each of the five single crochets in row 2 (see fig. 11), and turn your work. Continue to make as many rows as you like.

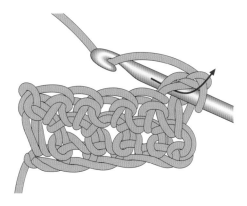

FIG. 11

Fastening Off

To fasten off, first cut the yarn from the ball, leaving a 5"-long strand extending from the loop on your hook. Then pull the entire loose end through the loop on the hook. Remove the hook and tug gently on the loose end until the loop is snug.

Learning More Stitches

 One delightful aspect of crocheting is its simplicity. Even the most intricate of crocheted fabrics is built on only a handful of basic stitches. There are infinite variations, of course, but all the stitches used to make the garments in this book are described in "All About Crochet." You certainly don't need to learn every stitch right away. Just turn to these pages whenever you need help.

An important note: Many of the illustrations in this section demonstrate how to make stitches in a base chain by inserting the hook through only the top loop of a chain stitch. Remember, however, that when you're working into a row other than a base chain, you'll insert your hook through *both* of the top two loops in the stitch unless the instructions direct you otherwise.

No matter what you're stitching, always insert the hook into the work from front to back unless the instructions tell you to work from back to front in order to create a special effect.

Slip Stitch (sl st)

A slip stitch has several functions. One of the most common is to join other stitches. To crochet a circular piece, for example, you can use the slip stitch to join the first stitch of the round to the last. This stitch is also used to join garment pieces (see "Slip-Stitch Seaming" on page 120) and to move your hook unobtrusively to another location in your work. In addition, the slip stitch is sometimes a part of another stitch (see "Loop-Stitch Variation" on page 105). Designer Nancy Brown calls this stitch a "nonstitch" because you don't include it when you count the stitches in a row.

1. Insert the hook into the next stitch.

2. YO, and pull the yarn through the stitch and the loop on the hook (see fig. 12).

FIG. 12

Chain Stitch (ch)

See "Making a Base Chain" on page 99.

Single Crochet (sc)

See "Crocheting the First Row" on page 100.

Half Double Crochet (hdc)

You can use the half-double-crochet stitch across an entire row or as a transitional stitch to carry your hook from a squat single crochet to a taller double crochet while keeping the edge of the fabric smooth. When the first stitch in a new row is a half double crochet, the instructions will usually tell you to work a two-stitch turning chain. When the half double crochet is the first stitch in a base chain, you usually work it into the third chain from the hook.

1. YO, and insert the hook into the next stitch.

2. YO, and pull the yarn through the stitch to the front of the work (see fig. 13).

FIG. 13

3. YO, and pull the yarn through all the loops on the hook (see fig. 14).

FIG. 14

Double Crochet (dc)

The double crochet is the most common of the crochet stitches that include multiple yarn wraps. When combined, these wraps (each made with a YO) create a vertical post. When the first stitch in a new row is a double crochet, the instructions will usually tell you to work a three-stitch turning chain. When the double crochet is the first stitch in a base chain, you usually work it into the fourth chain from the hook.

1. YO, and insert the hook into the next stitch (see fig. 15).

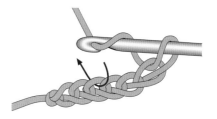

FIG. 15

2. YO, and pull the yarn through the stitch to the front of the work.

3. YO, and pull the yarn through 2 of the loops on the hook (see fig. 16).

FIG. 16

4. YO, and pull the yarn through the 2 remaining loops on the hook (see figs. 17 and 18).

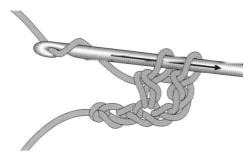

FIG. 17

FIG. 18

Treble Crochet (tr)

Once you master the double crochet, the treble is a breeze. This stitch has an additional YO at the start, so it's just a bit taller than the double crochet. When the first stitch in a new row is a treble crochet, the instructions will usually tell you to work a four-stitch turning chain. When the treble crochet is the first stitch in a base chain, you usually work it into the fifth chain from the hook.

1. YO twice, and insert the hook into the next stitch (see fig. 19).

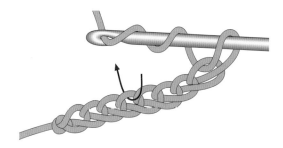

FIG. 19

2. YO, and pull the hook through the stitch to the front of the work.

3. YO, and pull the yarn through 2 of the loops on the hook (see fig. 20).

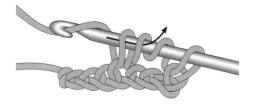

FIG. 20

4. YO, and pull the yarn through 2 of the loops on the hook (see fig. 21).

FIG. 21

5. YO, and pull the yarn through 2 of the loops on the hook (see figs. 22 and 23).

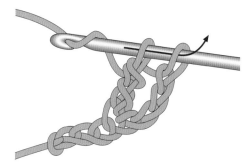

FIG. 22

FIG. 23

Reverse Single Crochet (rsc)

As its name implies, the reverse single-crochet stitch, which is often used to edge hems and necklines, is just a single crochet worked backwards along a row. Because you work a row of reverse single crochet from left to right, you don't turn your work before starting the row.

1. Insert the hook into the next stitch to the right (see fig. 24).

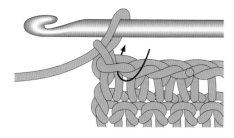

FIG. 24

2. YO, from right to left (this is easiest if you twist your hook so that its head is face down), and pull the loop to the front of the work (see fig. 25).

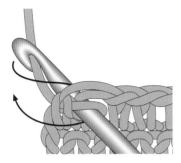

FIG. 25

3. Your hook should now be horizontal and pointing to the left. YO, and pull the yarn through the 2 loops on the hook (see fig. 26).

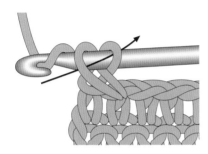

FIG. 26

Extended Single Crochet (esc)

The extended single-crochet stitch is taller than a single crochet, but it doesn't have a vertical post like the double crochet. When the first stitch in a row is an extended single crochet, the instructions will usually tell you to work one chain stitch for the turning chain.

1. Insert the hook into the next stitch.

2. YO, and pull the yarn to the front of the work.

3. YO, and pull the yarn through 1 loop on the hook (see fig. 27).

FIG. 27

4. YO, and pull the yarn through 2 loops on the hook (see fig. 28).

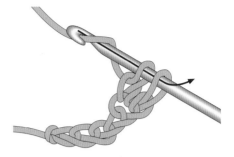

FIG. 28

Loop-Stitch Variation

Also called the fur stitch, the loop stitch is a lot of fun. In essence, it's made by adding yarn loops to a single crochet stitch. The loops end up on the side of the fabric that faces away from you during stitching. Because you want these stitches to appear on the outside (or right side) of your garment, you make them when the inside (or wrong side) of the fabric is facing you. You may be familiar with the type of loop stitch that has only one loop. Nancy Nehring's version, presented here, is fluffier.

To maintain an accurate stitch count, the rows before and after loop stitching must be worked in a specific manner (see the pattern entry on page 89).

1. Insert the hook through only the back loop of the next stitch.

2. YO, and pull the yarn through the stitch to the front of the work.

3. Insert your index finger in the loop, and adjust the loop to slightly less than 1" in height. Drop the loop from the hook, but keep it on your finger (see fig. 29).

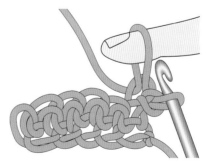

FIG. 29

4. YO (make sure the hook and yarn are in front of the loop on your finger, not behind it), and pull the yarn through the loop on the hook to make a slip stitch (see fig. 30).

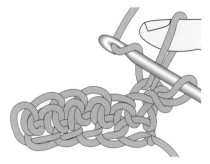

FIG. 30

5. Remove your finger from the loop.

6. You made the first loop into the back half (or back loop) of a stitch in the previous row. Now you're going to make another loop, this time into the front half (or front loop) of the same stitch in the previous row. Insert the hook through only the front loop of the same single crochet that you just worked into (see fig. 31). Then repeat steps 2–5 to complete this stitch.

FIG. 31

7. Continue making back- and front-loop stitches to complete a row, tugging each loop that you pull up in order to tighten the slip stitch. (Loops must be "set," or they'll unravel.) When you're finished, shake the work to fluff the loops.

Building Your Skills

Creating gorgeous crocheted fabric is simply a matter of making stitches, sometimes in rows and sometimes in rounds. (Only a few of the sweaters in this book include rounds.) Many of the patterns in *Crocheted Sweaters* transform ordinary stitches into extraordinary fabric by varying the basic stitches described in the previous pages.

Consider, for example, the interest that you can add to a piece of crocheted fabric just by alternating groups of single and double crochet. This simple pattern adds subtle wavy lines to the body of "Out of the Box" (see page 68). Alternatively, you can create instant drama by making a minor change to one basic stitch. For example, by working a double crochet around the post of a stitch in the row below (the row beneath the one you just stitched), you can create a deep ribbed effect. Toss in some single crochets, and you have the stylish Basketweave pattern. Both the Rib pattern and Basketweave pattern are featured in "Part of the Crew" on page 32.

Some of the patterns in this book may seem intimidating at first, but when you break them down into their component stitches, they're really quite simple. The same holds true for shaping crocheted fabric so that it isn't just a square or rectangle. A few decreases and increases repeated over several rows make all the difference (see "Decreasing and Increasing Stitches" on pages 111–112).

Working in Rows

If you followed the instructions in "Crocheting Your First Swatch" (see pages 98–101), you've already worked in rows. The sweater instructions will let you know how many stitches to make in your base chain, how to make the first and subsequent rows, and how many stitches each turning chain requires.

At the start of a row, the instructions may also include the abbreviation "RS" or "WS." Respectively, these stand for "right side" (the surface that shows when you wear the garment) and "wrong side" (the inside of the garment). These notations tell you which side of the work you're looking at as you stitch across that row. You'll only see these abbreviations when it's important for you to know which side of the piece you're working on.

When the instructions tell you to work into the "next stitch," they're directing you to the next stitch in the row that you just completed (the previous row). At the start of a row, the instructions may tell you to work into the "first" stitch instead. This is the stitch that's closest to the hook—the same stitch that the turning chain you just made is built on—in the row you just completed.

Sometimes a pattern may require you to work beneath the row you just created. For example, as you stitch row 3, you may need to work your stitches into row 1 instead of row 2. When this is the case, the instructions will include the phrase "in the row below."

In some cases, you work stitches into horizontal bars or vertical posts in the previous row rather than into the top loops of stitches in the row you just worked. There's more on this in a moment.

Turning Chains (tch)

As you already know, a turning chain serves to raise your hook up to the height of the row that you're about to work and consists of one or more chain stitches. Use figure 32 as a guide to the number of stitches that turning chains usually require. For a row that starts with a double-crochet stitch, for example, the turning chain typically consists of three chain stitches. Crochet instructions usually tell you the number of chains you need to make: typically one for a single crochet, two for a half double crochet, three for a double crochet, and so on.

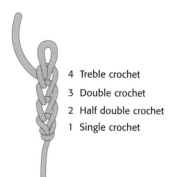

4 Treble crochet
3 Double crochet
2 Half double crochet
1 Single crochet

FIG. 32

In some crochet instructions, the turning chain appears at the end of a row; you make the chain stitches before turning the work. In others, the turning chain appears at the start of the new row. All instructions, however, tell you the number of chain stitches to make, even if they don't identify them as the turning chain.

Never second-guess a designer by adding your own turning chain.

In this book, the turning chains are usually positioned at the start of each row. You make your very first turning chain at the end of the base chain by making the first stitch of row 1 a specified number of chain stitches away from the hook. The chain stitches you skip are your turning chain for this row.

Thanks to the turning chain, it's all too easy to end up with too many or too few stitches in a row. When I was a beginner, instead of stitching squares of fabric, I always ended up creating upside-down triangles; my work got wider with each row. Why? Because I was inadvertently adding stitches. First, I would make a turning chain. Then I would work stitches into every stitch in the previous row and one stitch into the top of the turning chain (see fig. 33).

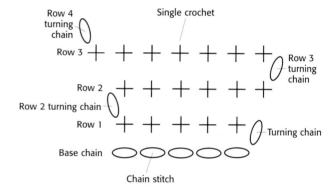

FIG. 33

Now I know better. I make my turning chain, skip the "first" stitch of the row that I just completed (the stitch that my turning chain is built on), stitch across the row, and make another stitch into the top of the turning chain of the previous row (see figs. 34 and 35), treating the turning chain as a stitch. You can do the same.

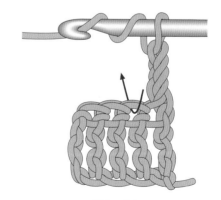

FIG. 34

TURNING CHAIN COUNTED AS A STITCH

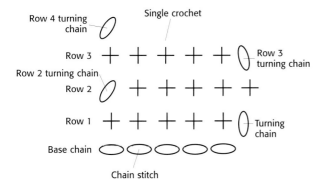

FIG. 35

There's one exception to this rule: the turning chain made when the first stitch is a single crochet (see fig. 36). In this case, you ignore the turning chain rather than count it as a stitch; you work into the first stitch in each row (the one the turning chain is built on) and not into the turning chain at the end.

TURNING CHAIN NOT COUNTED AS A STITCH

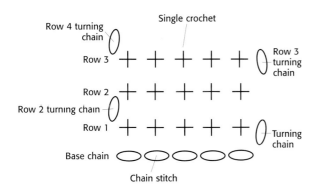

FIG. 36

In rare situations, some crochet instructions may tell you to count the turning chain for a single crochet as a stitch, and work the first single crochet into the next, rather than the first, stitch. The instructions in this book always tell you what to do.

Working in Rounds

Working in rounds is the process of creating circles, pentagons, squares, and other interesting shapes. The traditional granny squares in "Granny's Attic" (see page 40), for example, are worked in rounds.

As with rows, the starting point of a round is usually a slip knot, followed by chain stitches. The first round often consists of only a few chains, and the first chain stitch is joined to the last with a slip stitch (see figs. 37 and 38).

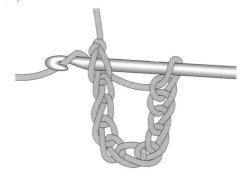

FIG. 37

FIG. 38

Once you've created this small circle, you typically work one or more chain stitches to lift the hook to the height of the second round, in the same way that you make turning chains when you work in rows. (For a spiral effect, you omit the slip stitch and the beginning chain at the start of each round.) Next, you create the second round by working into the first circle of chain stitches. Then you join the end of the second round to its beginning with a slip stitch, "lift" the hook again with a beginning chain, and continue with the next round. Pattern instructions define the size of the first circle, how to join its ends, and the stitches required to make each subsequent round.

Working in the Front or Back Loop

Ordinarily, you make crochet stitches by inserting the hook into the top two loops of the specified stitch. A stitch may be "anchored," however, in only one of these two loops: the front loop (see fig. 39) or the back loop. Jane Snedden Peever effectively uses this treatment to imitate a knitted rib pattern in "Double Take" (see page 50).

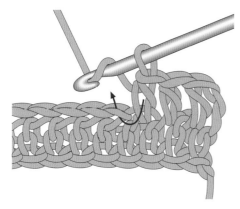

FIG. 39

Working around a Post

A post is the vertical stack that results from the multiple YOs you make when you create a tall stitch such as the double crochet. When a pattern requires working around the post, you do so from the front or the back.

For a front post, you insert the hook, from front to back, on the right side of the post, immediately below the two loops that you'd normally work into. (Depending on the stitch that you're making, you may need to YO first.) Then you swing the hook behind the post and forward to the front of the work, on the left side of the post (see fig. 40). In crochet instructions, this process appears as "FP" (the abbreviation for front post), followed by the stitch abbreviation. FPDC, for example, stands for front post double crochet.

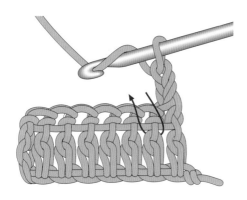

FIG. 40

Next, you YO and pull the yarn back around the post, to the front of the work on the right side of the post. Then you complete the stitch in the usual fashion.

As its name suggests, a back-post stitch (abbreviated as "BP") is worked by inserting the hook on the right side of the post, through the fabric from back to front, and bringing the hook to the left side of the post, from front to back.

Front- and back-post stitches are sometimes worked into the previous row. At other times, they're worked into the row below; in other words, if you're on row 3 and making a front- or back-post stitch in the row below, you work around the post of a stitch in row 1.

The trick to making a front- or back-post double-crochet stitch is setting up the stitches the first time that they're called for in a pattern. As an example, the work might start with two rows of plain stitching. On the next row, the front- or back-post double-crochet stitch is worked into the row below, while the next stitch of the pattern is made in the previous row (the row you just worked). Figure 41 illustrates how to work an FPDC followed by a single crochet, as required for the Left Cross Cable pattern in "Aran Classic" (see page 14) and Basketweave pattern in "Part of the Crew" (see page 32). Don't worry if the completed FPDC appears to be in front of (to the left of) the stitch that you work into the previous row; it's supposed to! Once worked, the FPDC and BPDC stand out from the surface, so it's easy to work into (and around) them in subsequent rows.

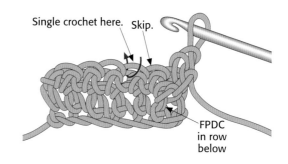

Single crochet here. Skip.

FPDC in row below

FIG. 41

Working around a Chain-Space

You'll encounter this situation when you're doing open-work and other lace-like patterns. In the previous row, there are one or more chain stitches that make a gap or loop. Each gap or loop is called a "chain-space." In the new row, the pattern may call for you to make a stitch in the chain that makes up the chain-space. This is called working around the chain-space.

To start, YO if required for your stitch. Insert the hook, from front to back, underneath the chain. YO, and bring the yarn to the front of the work. Finish the stitch in the usual manner. You have just worked around the chain-space. Complete the stitch in the usual manner (see fig. 42).

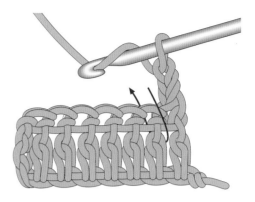

FIG. 43

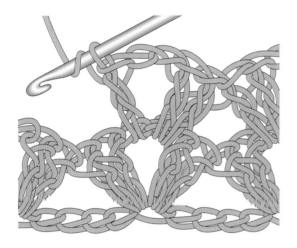

FIG. 42

Working between Stitches

To work between stitches, ignore the two loops at the top of the stitch, and insert the hook through the larger hole between the posts, from front to back. Remember to YO as required to create the new stitch, before and after hook insertion (see fig. 43). Finish the stitch in the usual manner.

Decreasing and Increasing Stitches

Designers often shape garment pieces so their finished sweaters will fit in a particular way. For example, they may cinch a waist and flare out the hips, set in sleeves to sit at the tops of the shoulders, or curve a front neckline so it doesn't bunch up against the throat.

Garments can be shaped by adding special pieces (the side panels in "Tokyo Vest" on page 58 are good examples), but designers usually shape their garments by working more or fewer stitches in one or more rows. The instructions in *Crocheted Sweaters* provide instructions for increases and decreases whenever they're needed.

For the simplest, single-stitch increase, you simply work two stitches into one stitch in the previous row.

To make a single-stitch decrease anywhere along a row of dense fabric, you work one stitch into the next two stitches. The instructions specify the stitch to make, followed by the decrease abbreviation "2tog." For example, "sc2tog" (single crochet two together) means that you work one single crochet into the next two stitches. Instructions for common decrease stitches follow.

Single-Crochet Decrease (sc2tog)

Insert the hook through the next stitch, YO, and pull the yarn through the stitch. Then (this is where you decrease by picking up an extra stitch) insert the hook into the *next* stitch, YO, and pull the yarn to the front of the work. YO, and pull the yarn through all the loops on the hook.

Half-Double-Crochet Decrease (hdc2tog)

YO, insert the hook into the next stitch, YO, and pull the yarn through the stitch. YO, insert the hook into the *next* stitch, YO, and pull the yarn through the stitch. YO, and pull the yarn through the three loops on the hook.

Double-Crochet Decrease (dc2tog)

YO, insert the hook into the next stitch, YO, and pull the yarn through the stitch. YO, and pull the yarn through two loops. YO, insert the hook into the *next* stitch, YO, and pull the yarn through the stitch. YO, pull the yarn through two loops, YO, and pull the yarn through all three loops.

At the end of a row, the easiest way to make a multiple-stitch decrease is to omit working the last stitch or stitches. At the beginning of a row, you can decrease by slip stitching into the specified number of stitches. There are other ways to work decreases in filet crochet, openwork, and other lace-like stitches. All multiple-stitch decreases are fully explained in the sweater instructions.

Adding New Yarn

You'll add a new strand of yarn whenever a yarn ball or skein runs out, you want to change yarn colors, or you start an edging.

When you're working a garment piece, the best place to start new yarn is at the beginning or end of a row because you can hide the yarn ends inside the finished garment. Don't tie the old and new yarn ends together; this makes an ugly lump! Instead, drop the old yarn, and use the start of the new ball or skein to make the last YO in a stitch, leaving a 5"-long tail of new yarn beyond the stitching (see fig. 44). Make sure the yarn ends are on the wrong side of the fabric. When you start new yarn in the middle of the work, also make sure the yarn ends are on the wrong side.

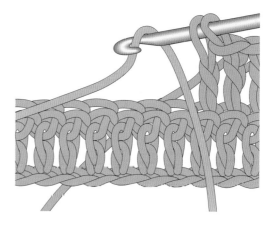

FIG. 44

When you're making a dense fabric, you can work right over the old and new yarn ends as you make the next few stitches. However, I prefer to thread each end onto a blunt needle and weave it in and out of the stitches on the wrong side after the garment piece is made.

When you start an edging, you usually don't have a loop on your hook, so make a slip knot on the hook with the new yarn. Then make the first stitch in the usual manner (see fig. 45). For the first and subsequent edging stitches, YO if required, insert the hook into the fabric from front to back, YO, and pull the loop to the front.

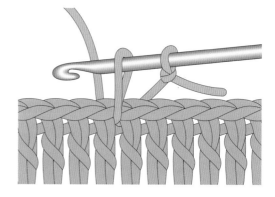

FIG. 45

Understanding Crochet Instructions

At first glance, crochet instructions can look rather difficult. And their presentation varies, depending on which book or magazine you're reading. Once you know how to interpret instructions, however, they're quite simple, and they almost always include the same elements, no matter where they're published. In this section, you'll learn how to read and use the instructions in this book, and in very short order, you'll be crocheting like a pro.

Sizing

"Sizing" is usually the first entry in any set of crochet instructions and almost always includes two important elements. The first is often a "To fit bust" line, which includes the dimensions for all the different sizes embedded in the sweater instructions. (Crochet instructions actually include several sets of instructions—one set for each size.) Following is a typical example.

> To fit bust: 31½ (34¼, 37¼, 41, 43¼)"

The first number, 31½", represents the smallest size, extra-small—in this case, a body that is 31½" around the front and back at the full bust. The numbers within the parentheses are the bust measurements for subsequent sizes. In this example, small is 34¼", medium is 37¼", large is 41", and extra-large is 43¼".

Measure yourself around your full bust, and compare your measurement to one of the numbers in the entry. If your measurement falls between two numbers, shift to the lower size if you're lean or to the larger size if you're shapelier.

Suppose your bust measures 34". The closest number in the entry is 34¼"—or small. Note that this number is the second one listed and appears first within the parentheses. Now you know that the set of instructions you need to follow always appears second—and first within the parentheses. For example, if you see "Chain 62 (68, 74, 80, 86, 92)" in the instructions, you'll make a 68-stitch chain. To avoid confusion, highlight all the numbers for your size wherever parentheses appear in the instructions.

In many instructions, there will be places where one measurement, stitch count, or row count applies to all of the sizes. In this case, the parentheses are omitted and only one number appears.

The second important element in "Sizing" provides at least one of the measurements of the finished garment, often the "Finished bust," as in the example that follows.

Finished bust: 36 (40, 44, 48, 52)"

If you're a size small, then the exterior circumference of your finished sweater at the bust will be 40".

The difference between the "To fit bust" and "Finished bust" measurements indicates how snugly or loosely your sweater will fit. These extra inches (called "ease") help define the sweater's look. Never choose a size by matching your body measurement to the finished bust size, or you'll end up with a skintight sweater! For more information on ease, see pages 121–122.

Schematics

Schematics (see page 18 for examples) are drawings of the pieces that make up a sweater. They provide the details of the shaping, such as the depth and length of the neckline; and they include the critical dimensions, rounded to the nearest ¼", for every size. You use schematics to check your sweater pieces as you crochet them.

You can also use schematics to figure out how well a sweater will fit you. Start by finding an existing sweater that fits you well, with a shape similar to the one you want to make. Lay the sweater flat and measure the same areas for which measurements are given on the schematics for the new sweater. If the sweater measurements match or are close to those on the schematics, you'll probably like the fit of the new sweater. If they aren't close, you may want to adjust your new sweater's fit (see "Perfecting Fit" on pages 121–123).

Schematics can also be very helpful when you want to make sure that the sleeves of a sweater will be the perfect length for you. My friend Louise Cutting, a sewing expert, taught me a valuable lesson about sleeve

measurements: Lengths can be deceiving. The shoulder-to-wrist measurement for size small, for example, is 23¼", yet a 15"-long sleeve may fit perfectly if the sweater is a drop-shoulder style. Why? Because the body drops over the shoulders and down the tops of the arms, and the sleeves are attached below the arm and shoulder hinge.

To make sure the sleeves of a sweater will fit you, start by figuring out your desired sleeve length. Measure from the base of your neck, at center back, along the shoulder on the same side, over your slightly bent elbow, and down to your wrist. (I like my sleeves to end between my wrist and the base of my thumb, so that's where my measurement ends.) Write down this length.

Now turn to the sweater's schematics. Find the width of the sweater's back, and divide it in half. Next, add the total length shown on the sleeve schematic. Subtract ¼" from the result to compensate for the length you'll lose when you seam the sleeve to the body (see fig. 46). Compare this finished garment measurement with the desired length that you recorded earlier. To adjust the sleeve length, see "Altering Length" on page 123.

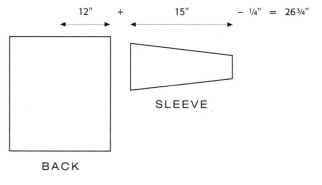

FIG. 46

Materials

Each set of garment instructions in this book includes a "Materials" entry. An example follows.

> Lion Brand *MicroSpun* (100% microfiber acrylic: 2½ ozs./70 g; 168 yds./151 m): 7 (8, 9, 10, 11) balls of #148 Turquoise (MC); and 1 ball each of #186 Mango (A), #194 Lime (B), #146 Fuchsia (C), and #158 Buttercup (D)
> F/5 (4 mm) crochet hook

The first part of this entry lists the yarns used in the sweater. The name of the manufacturer, distributor, or brand is followed by the name of the yarn—in this case, *MicroSpun*. The fiber content, weight, and length are provided next. Take this yarn information with you when you visit the yarn shop.

The list of numbers that comes before the word "balls" (or "skeins" or "hanks") tells you how much yarn is required for the main color (MC), depending on the sweater size you've decided to make. In our example, a medium-sized sweater requires nine balls of the main color, which is #148 Turquoise. The main color (or body) yarn is used more than any other yarn in the sweater, usually for the background.

When other yarns are required, they're listed—along with the number of balls or skeins needed—after the main color, and are given letter designations: "A," "B," "C," and so forth.

The next line provides the suggested crochet hook size, in both U.S. and metric. Any additional items required to make a particular sweater are listed after the hook size, but the "Materials" entry doesn't include the general-purpose tools and supplies that you'll always need to have on hand.

Featured Stitches

This entry lists all the stitches in the sweater, along with their standard abbreviations (see "Stitching Instructions" on pages 116–117). An example follows.

> Back post double crochet (BPDC); see page 110
> Chain (ch); see page 99
> Front post double crochet (FPDC); see page 110

Gauge

I once gave a presentation called "Skeletons in My Closet" to a group of Canadian knitters. The audience roared with laughter as I showed them one gargantuan sweater after another. One was so huge I could wrap it around my less-than-lithe body twice. Why were these sweaters so large? Because I crochet loosely, but the garment instructions I used were written for the average crocheter, who works tighter stitches than I do. Unless I adjust my gauge (or yarn tension), my loose stitches

result in oversize sweaters. Not until I started editing pattern instructions did I realize how important it is to work in the specified gauge.

The gauge of a sweater is measured as the number of stitches and rows per inch and is the result of hook size, yarn thickness, and the tightness of the stitching. Gauge can make a tremendous difference to how well a garment fits. When your gauge matches the instructions, your sweater will fit as the designer intended: The sleeves will be the right length, the armholes will feel comfortable, and the shoulder seams won't rest at your elbows or neck! If your gauge differs from the designer's by even one stitch, however, the results can be disastrous, especially when you're working with a heavy yarn.

A typical "Gauge" entry follows.

> 12 sts and 14 rows to 4" in Basketweave pattern, with H/8 (5 mm) hook

In the language of crochet, this means that a 4" square of the designer's finished sweater—in this case, an area stitched in a Basketweave pattern—will be twelve stitches wide and fourteen rows tall.

You don't have to crochet an entire sweater to ensure that your stitch and row counts match those in the instructions, or to find out that they don't. Take a shortcut, instead, by creating a gauge swatch before you begin your sweater.

A gauge swatch is a piece of crocheted fabric, about 6" square, that you work in the yarn and stitch or pattern specified in the instructions. With this gauge swatch, you will measure a 4"-square area in the center to determine your gauge. Working a swatch rarely takes more than thirty minutes and allows you to compare your own gauge with the designer's.

Start by pulling out the yarn that's specified in the "Materials" list for your project. Next, chain the number of stitches specified in the "Gauge" entry by using the hook listed there or in the "Materials" list. Then make enough extra chains (half the number of stitches listed) to create a finished swatch about 6" wide. To make a swatch for our twelve-stitch example, you'd start with a chain that's eighteen stitches long.

Turn at the end of the chain and work across it to make row 1. The "Gauge" entry either specifies the stitch to use for this and subsequent rows, or lets you know that the gauge is worked in a specific pattern. (Look for the pattern entry in the sweater instructions for row-by-row guidance.) To make the pattern repeat work in the swatch, you may need to adjust the number of stitches in the base chain (see the next section). Continue working additional rows until your swatch is about 6" tall; then fasten off the work (see "Fastening Off" on page 101).

Pin the outer edges of your finished swatch to a flat surface such as an ironing board or a piece of cardboard. Make sure that the swatch is square, or your row and stitch counts won't be accurate. Don't stretch the work. Next, either use a ruler to measure a 4" square in the center of the swatch, or center the 4"-square opening of a tension gauge measure on top of the swatch. Then count the rows and stitches inside the 4"-square area. When you use a tension gauge measure, you can tell immediately if your swatch is distorted because the rows won't be parallel to the edges of the plastic frame.

The moment of truth has arrived. If the number of stitches and rows in your swatch match the "Gauge" entry, your gauge matches the designer's. If the numbers don't match, work a new swatch with a different size crochet hook; use a smaller hook to increase the number of stitches or a larger hook for fewer stitches. Adjusting your stitch size by using a different hook will probably increase or decrease the number of rows as needed. If you can't match your row gauge to the designer's, you can work more or fewer rows as you make your sweater pieces (see "Altering Length" and "Altering Width" on page 123).

Patterns

In this book, when instructions for a garment include a stitch combination that's worked over several stitches or rows, a separate pattern entry is provided. This entry, which explains how to make one repeat of the pattern, starts by telling you the number of stitches you need to add to the base chain to "set up" the repeat and make the first turning chain. Here's an example:

> Multiple of 4 sts + 3 (also add 1 st for
> base chain)

To make a gauge swatch in this pattern, you must chain a number that's divisible by four (the number of

stitches in the pattern repeat), add three more to set up the pattern in the row, and make one more stitch. The last stitch is only added if you're starting with a base chain. When you start the pattern in a piece of crocheted fabric that's already underway, the total stitches in the previous row need only be a multiple of four, plus three.

The rest of the pattern entry specifies the number and types of stitches and the number of rows required to make a single repeat.

In some situations, a pattern can't be started until one row is worked into the base chain. This row is called a "foundation row"; it isn't a part of the pattern, and it isn't repeated. The pattern instructions that follow this row walk you through all the rows required to complete one pattern repeat.

Fancy stitches and patterns aren't necessary when a sweater shape is especially interesting or when you're using a wonderful yarn. Some of the sweaters in this book are made with a single stitch, worked row after row. You won't find a "Pattern" entry in these sweater instructions.

Stitching Instructions

Now comes the fun part—the row-by-row instructions. These are provided separately for each garment piece. Don't panic when you take your first look at a set of crochet instructions! Think of them, instead, as written in code—a code that's easy to learn. As mentioned earlier, the abbreviations for the particular stitches used in a sweater are listed in the "Featured Stitches" entry. The instructions combine these stitch abbreviations with other standard abbreviations.

Unless you need to work a special edging, stitch into an existing garment edge, or make an unusual stitch, the instructions for each piece of your sweater will start with a specified number of chain stitches. These are followed by the instructions for row 1, which you work into the chain stitches. From this point onward, the instructions will guide you through every row or round of the sweater piece by listing the stitches in sequential order. Take a look at the following example.

> **Row 2:** Ch 3 (count as dc), dc in next st, *ch 1,
> sk 1 st, dc in next st*, rep from * to * to end.
> [20 (22, 24, 26, 28) sts]

Start this row with three chain stitches. These make up the turning chain for this row. The instructions tell you to pretend that the three-stitch turning chain is a double-crochet stitch. You'll find out why in a minute.

Now start making stitches into row 1. Don't work into the stitch that the turning chain is built on. Make one double crochet (dc) in the next stitch. (Unless they're chains, the number of stitches required is always placed before the stitch abbreviation.)

Next, you come to what's called a "repeat"—a combination of stitches that you must repeat across the row. In this book, repeats are enclosed in asterisks. You complete one repeat in this example by making one chain stitch, skipping one stitch in the previous row, and making one double crochet in the next stitch of the previous row.

An explanation of how to treat the repeat follows the second asterisk. In this example, you repeat the stitch combination to the end of the row, working the last stitch of the last repeat (a double crochet) into the turning chain of the previous row. Remember: When your turning chain counts as a stitch, you make the last stitch of the row in the turning chain of the previous row. When the last stitch isn't worked into the turning chain, the instructions will explain what to do.

The bracketed numbers represent the number of stitches made in that row. They appear at the end of any row where you might need to check your work: an increase or decrease row, for example, or the first row worked into a base chain. Since the instructions for that row told you to count the turning chain as a double-crochet stitch, it's included in the stitch count.

Common Terms

Crochet instructions make use of many abbreviated terms and phrases. Following are descriptions of the most common ones.

Across: Continue making stitches as directed along the row until you reach the specified stitch.

As; As for; Work as for: Make the new garment piece or row(s) by following the instructions to which you're directed.

Doubled yarn: Use two strands, handling them as if they were one.

alt	alternate
approx	approximately
beg	begin(ning)
blo	back loop only
BPDC(s)	back post double crochet(s)
cb3	3-stitch cable
ch(s)	chain(s)
ch-sp	chain-space
col	color
cont	continue(ing)
dc	double crochet
dc2tog	double crochet 2 together
dec	decrease(ing)
esc	extended single crochet
flo	front loop only
foll	follow(s)(ing)
FPDC(s)	front post double crochet(s)
hdc	half double crochet
hdc2tog	half double crochet 2 together
inc	increase(ing)
lp(s)	loop(s)
lsv	loop stitch variation
MC	main color
pat	pattern
rem	remaining
rep	repeat
rev	reverse(ing)
rnd(s)	round(s)
RS	right side(s)
rsc	reverse single crochet
sc	single crochet
sc2tog	single crochet 2 together
sk	skip
sl st	slip stitch
sp(s)	space(s)
st(s)	stitch(es)
tch	turning chain
tog	together
tr	treble crochet
WS	wrong side(s)
YO	yarn over

First stitch: This is the stitch that the turning chain is built on, in the row that you just completed.

In pat: Make the stitches and rows according to the pattern.

In pat as established: Work the next stitch or row that's required to maintain the existing pattern in the crocheted fabric.

Left (or right): Where a garment piece rests on your body when you wear the finished garment.

Multiple of: The number of rows or stitches in a pattern repeat.

Next stitch: The stitch that follows the first stitch at the beginning of the row, or any stitch right after the one you've just stitched.

Previous row: The row that you just completed. For example, if you're on row 5, the previous row is row 4.

Row below: The row underneath the previous row. For example, if you're on row 5, the row below is row 3.

Work even: Stitch to the end of the row (or work as many rows or inches as specified) without making any decreases or increases.

Work as for . . . to: Make the new garment piece or row(s) by following the instructions to which you are directed, up to—but not including—the section noted after "to."

Finishing

To finish a sweater, first you must sew in all the loose yarn ends on each garment piece (see "Adding New Yarn" on page 112). Then you may need to block each piece by using moisture to set its shape. Next comes assembling the pieces, a task that crocheters either love or loathe. If you find this stage tedious, pack your pieces off to a local yarn shop; many offer finishing services. You may also need to add edging (see page 120).

The "Finishing" entry usually indicates the order in which to join the pieces, where to stitch an edging if one is required, and may also include other details such as suitable seaming methods.

Blocking Sweater Pieces

The goal of blocking is to shape each garment piece to the dimensions provided in its schematic. Blocking provides a great opportunity to realign any rows that shifted off the straight and narrow during stitching.

Avoid blocking fluffy yarns or fibers that might be damaged by moisture or heat. (If you're unsure about blocking a particular yarn, ask for advice from an expert at a yarn shop.) Don't waste time blocking yarns with a high polyester or acrylic content; your sweater pieces will bounce back to their original shapes as soon as you remove the T-pins.

To steam-block a piece, first use T-pins to pin it to the blocking surface so that its width, length, and overall shape match the dimensions in the schematic. Be careful not to stretch the fabric out of shape. I often use a T-square or triangle to ensure that the rows and stitches are at right angles. Use a straightedge and ruler to check all measurements.

Next, hold an iron set to "steam" about ¼" above the crocheted fabric for a few seconds. Don't place the iron on the yarn! Give the steam enough time to penetrate the yarn fibers; then move on to the next spot until you've steamed the entire piece. Let the fabric dry thoroughly before removing the T-pins.

To wet-block a piece instead of steaming it, pin the piece to the blocking surface and cover it with a dampened towel. Leave the towel in place overnight, remove it the next day, and allow the piece to dry before removing the T-pins. Alternatively, you can spray the pinned sweater piece with water and then let it dry.

Joining Methods

Garment pieces are often assembled by joining them with a hand-sewn running stitch or with a crocheted slip stitch.

RUNNING-STITCH SEAMING

Use this method unless the instructions recommend another technique. Place the garment pieces with their right sides together, and align the edges that you plan to join. Next, thread a large, sharp-pointed needle with a long strand of yarn. To secure the end of the strand in the fabric, pull the yarn in and out through a few stitches in the wrong side of one of the pieces, at the start of the seam.

Insert the needle down through both fabric layers and bring it up again a short distance away, along the edges to be joined. Repeat this in-and-out motion along the length of the seam. Your stitch length will depend on your fabric. You don't want any gaps in the seamline, but avoid stitching so closely and tightly that the seamline draws in. My stitches are usually ¼" to ½" long.

When you're finished, secure the end of the yarn by pulling it in and out through several stitches on the wrong side of the fabric. Cut off the excess yarn tail.

SLIP-STITCH SEAMING

To join garment pieces with a slip stitch, first place them with their right sides together and align the edges to be joined. Next, place a slip knot on your crochet hook. Working between the first and the second stitch from the layered edge, insert the hook, from front to back, through both layers of the crocheted fabric. YO, and pull the loop through both fabric layers and the slip knot that's on the hook. Repeat this stitch along the edge, keeping your stitches loose enough to prevent the fabric from drawing up.

Edgings

Vertical or diagonal edges on crocheted fabric can be unstable or look unfinished. To stabilize edges or to add a decorative touch, many designers like to include edgings—one or more rows of stitching added to hems, sleeves, and/or necklines.

Perfecting Fit

When I was in my early twenties, a university instructor taught me something that radically changed my perception of bodies: There's no such thing as a "normal" shape. In fact, fit models—the gals whose measurements match the standards of a designer or manufacturer—are so rare that they're paid handsomely for their unique dimensions. It's no wonder that the rest of us sometimes have problems with the necks or sleeves of garments, even though our bust measurements may match those in the instructions.

The fit of crocheted sweaters, like their knitted cousins, is forgiving. In fact, you'll probably be safe if you bypass all the information in this section, match your bust measurement to the "To fit bust" entry for your sweater, and get to work. But if an excellent fit is as important to you as it is to me, read on.

Evaluating Ease

When crochet instructions offer both "To fit bust" and "Finished bust" measurements, you can estimate how loosely or tightly a garment will fit you. The difference between the two numbers is the amount of extra crocheted fabric that wraps around your body at the bust. For example, if your bust is 34" and the "Finished bust" measurement is 44", the sweater will probably be very loose fitting because its bust measurement is 10" larger than yours. I say "probably" because the thickness of the yarn does influence the fit. Finished measurements are taken on the outside of a sweater, so a bulky yarn, which yields a thicker fabric, leaves less space inside the sweater than a yarn that isn't bulky.

The instructions for every sweater in this book include a description of the sweater's fit. The "Ease Guidelines" chart below shows how this fit information is determined. Keep in mind, however, that the amount of ease in a sweater may not be exactly the same as the measurements listed in this table because a designer may have added more or less fabric to achieve a specific look.

EASE GUIDELINES

Close Fitting	Fitted	Semifitted	Loose Fitting	Very Loose Fitting
Up to 3"	Up to 4"	Up to 5"	Up to 8"	More than 8"

If a garment has less than 6" of ease at the bust and hips and is worked in a bulky yarn, it probably won't look good on you! To be safe, make sure a bulky-yarn garment has 8" or more of ease.

Choosing Your Size

The designers of the sweaters in this book used the measurements shown in the chart below as the starting point for their creations, so every sweater is built on a specific body frame for each size.

How can the information in this table help you? First, you can bank on the fact that any sweater in this book that's described as ending at the hip will always stop at roughly the same spot. And long sleeves will all stop at the same location, regardless of the pattern. So, if the sleeves of one sweater are 1" too long or short for you, the sleeves of any other sweater will probably need to be adjusted by the same amount. Just add (or subtract) the difference between the arm length in the table and your own desired arm length—in inches or rows—to (or from) the sleeve length of your sweater.

Second, just because your dimensions differ from the standardized ones in this table doesn't mean that your sweater can't fit well. If you have trouble spots, you can use this table to help you determine an appropriate size by going beyond your full bust measurement—and then fine-tune a sweater's fit before you start stitching.

Start by having a friend measure the areas of your body that are listed in the table. Jot down the numbers in the empty column. Don't cheat! Then, in the chart, find the underbust, high hip width, full hip width, and back neck to waist measurements that most closely correspond to your own. The column in which most of these measurements fall represents your size.

The spots where your measurements differ are the places where you may need to add or subtract stitches or rows. If a sweater is shaped at the waist, for example, the

BODY MEASUREMENTS

	Your Measurements	X-Small	Small	Medium	Large	X-Large
Widths						
Full bust		31½"	34¼"	37¼"	41"	43¼"
Underbust		27¾"	29½"	32½"	36¼"	38½"
Waist		26½"	29¾"	32½"	37"	39½"
High hip		33¾"	36½"	39"	43½"	45½"
Full hip		35½"	37¾"	40"	43½"	44¾"
Wrist circumference		6"	6¼"	6¾"	6¾"	6¾"
Lengths						
Back neck to high hip		19½"	19½"	20"	20½"	20¾"
Back neck to full hip		22½"	23"	23¾"	24½"	26"
Back neck to waist		15¾"	16"	16½"	16¾"	26"
Shoulder length (base of neck to shoulder/arm joint)		5"	5¼"	5¼"	5¾"	5½"
Arm length (shoulder/arm joint to wrist)		22¾"	23¼"	23¾"	24¼"	24¾"

"Body Measurements" chart tells you that in size medium, the shaped area is 16½" below the prominent bone at the base of the back neck. If your full bust is size medium, but your waist is 17¼" away from the base of the back neck, just start the waist shaping ¾" lower than called for in the instructions.

Garments are usually sized for B-cup busts. If you take an A cup or a C cup, you may want to use the underbust measurement instead of the full bust when choosing the size that's best for you. A sweater size based on a full bust measurement may very well fit you, depending on the amount of ease in the design, but sometimes an unaltered sweater with sufficient fabric through the full bust for a C cup may not look good elsewhere. For example, the shoulder seams may be too low on the upper arms, and the waist may be too long. Similarly, on an A-cup figure, an unaltered sweater based on a full bust size may end up with too much fabric around the front torso.

Altering Length

If your body-length measurements don't match one size in the "Body Measurements" chart, remember that crocheted sweaters are forgiving. Alterations may not be necessary. You can certainly adjust the length of the body or sleeves, though, by making more or fewer rows than called for in the pattern.

How do you calculate the number of rows to add or subtract? Here's where the gauge information comes into play. Suppose you need to shorten the sleeve by 2", and the gauge is sixteen stitches and twenty rows to 4". Divide twenty by four, and you now know there are five rows to every inch of length. To shorten the body or sleeve by 2", just work ten fewer rows. (Until you're comfortable making alterations, avoid tackling length adjustments in a garment that's worked in vertical rows.)

Some of the sweaters in this book feature sleeves that are stitched from the shoulder down to the wrist. To shorten or lengthen these sleeves, just keep stitching until you reach the desired length. Then fasten off your work.

Traditional sleeve patterns are worked from wrist to shoulder. For these types of sleeves, make the adjustment near the start of your stitching. To shorten the sleeve, work fewer rows in the lower arm area, before the sleeve-width increases begin.

Some sleeves and hems are finished with an edging. In most cases, a single edging row won't affect the length much, but a deeper edging might. Work a swatch to determine the depth of the edging, and take this depth into account when you adjust the length.

If you're a beginner, I don't advise tackling row adjustments on shaped sweaters; you need to be comfortable working with gauges before you can make successful alterations of this kind. Changing row counts in areas that have increases and decreases for the armholes, waist, and neckline can be challenging.

Altering Width

The ease in a sweater sometimes solves body-width problems, so you may not need to make any alterations. Width adjustments can be difficult when a sweater includes side shaping or a pattern. On the other hand, adjusting body width is easy if the sides of the sweater are straight and if you don't have to worry about changing a pattern. Just use the "Gauge" entry to calculate the number of stitches to add or subtract in each row. Divide the number of stitches in the gauge by the number of inches to determine the number of stitches per inch of width. Then multiply by the number of inches you want to add or subtract. One warning here: Keep in mind that altering width will change the finished width of the shoulders on your sweater. They'll be wider if you add stitches and narrower if you subtract them. You may need to adjust the sleeve length if the sweater has drop shoulders (see page 114 for more information).

Don't try to alter sleeve width until you've had some practice crocheting sweaters. This adjustment often interferes with the way the sleeve fits into the armhole.

Wrapping Up

A Visual Guide to Featured Yarns

Sooner or later, you'll fall in love with a spectacular yarn and want to use it to make a sweater in this book. Or you'll want to start stitching right away, but you won't be able to find the yarn specified in the sweater instructions. With the information on these pages, you can successfully substitute one yarn for another.

Compare the photo of the featured yarn with the one you'd like to try. The two yarns must have the same characteristics because crocheted fabric can look very different when stitched in yarns that aren't similar. In a smooth yarn, for example, the fabric for "Lightning Strike" would be full of holes.

Aran Classic (see page 14)
Patons *Decor;* 75% acrylic, 25% wool
3½ ozs./100 g; 210 yds./192 m

Beginner's Luck (see page 8)
Lion Brand *Chenille Thick & Quick;* 91% acrylic, 9% rayon
5 ozs./140 g; 94 yds./86 m

Bright Idea (see page 79)
Lion Brand *MicroSpun;* 100% microfiber acrylic
2½ ozs./70 g; 168 yds./151 m

Cat's Meow (see page 36)
Adriafil *Stars A & S;* 50% viscose, 50% nylon
1¾ ozs./50 g; 71 yds./65 m

Double Stripes (see page 19)
Berroco *Cotton Twist;* 70% mercerized cotton, 30% rayon
1¾ ozs./50 g; 85 yds./77 m

Double Take (see page 50)
Reynolds *Lopi;* 100% wool
3½ ozs./100 g; 109 yds./100 m

Evening Shade (see page 28)
Filatura Di Crosa *Millefilli Fine;* 100% cotton
1¾ ozs./50 g; 136½ yds./123 m

Fall Forward (see page 76)
Cascade *Pastaza;* 50% llama, 50% wool
3½ ozs./100 g; 132 yds./120 m

Granny's Attic (see page 40)
Skacel *Fortissima*; 75% virgin wool, 25% nylon
1¾ ozs./50 g; 229 yds./210 m

Homespun Hug (see page 45)
Lion Brand *Homespun*; 98% acrylic, 2% polyester
6 ozs./170 g; 185 yds./168 m

Ins and Outs (see page 54)
Red Heart *Soft*; 100% acrylic
5 ozs./140 g; 328 yds./295 m

Bernat *Illusions*; 90% acrylic, 10% nylon
5 ozs./140 g; 195 yds./113 m

Lightning Strike (see page 84)
Filatura Cervinia *Geisha*; 100% microfiber
1¾ ozs./50 g; 76 yds./70 m

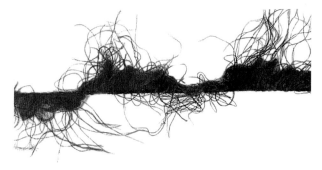

Loopy Idea (see page 88)
Skacel *Charming*; 40% cotton, 25% acrylic, 17% metallic,
10% polyester, 8% nylon
1¾ ozs./50 g; 104 yds./94 m

Out of the Box (see page 68)
Briggs & Little *Heritage*; 100% wool
4 ozs./113 g; 215 yds./196 m

Part of the Crew (see page 32)
Briggs & Little *Heritage*; 100% wool
4 ozs./113 g; 215 yds./196 m

Snug Hug Tank Top (see page 11)
Trendsetter *Dancer*; 57% polyester, 43% polyamid
1¾ ozs./50 g; 65 yds./59 m

Summer Breeze (see page 63)
Skacel *Riviera*; 45% cotton, 30% linen, 25% rayon
1¾ ozs./50 g; 110 yds./100 m

Surf and Turf (see page 72)
Tahki *Cotton Classic*; 100% cotton
1¾ ozs./50 g; 108 yds./97 m

Tokyo Vest (see page 58)
Skacel *Paradiso*; 60% cotton, 30% acrylic, 10% nylon
1¾ ozs./50 g; 110 yds./100 m

Skacel *Fortissima*; 75% cotton, 25% nylon
1¾ ozs./50 g; 231 yds./210 m

Two-Way Tee (see page 24)
Brown Sheep *Cotton Fleece*; 80% cotton, 20% merino wool
3½ ozs./100 g; 215 yds./196 m

Hook Sizes

PLASTIC, ALUMINUM, & WOOD HOOKS

U.S.	Metric	U.K.
B/1	2.5	12
C/2	3	11
D/3	3.25	10
E/4	3.5	9
F/5	4	8
G/6	4.25	7
7	4.5	6
H/8	5	5
I/9	5.5	4
J/10	6	3
K/10.5	7	-
L/11	8	-
M/13	9	-
N/15	10	-
P/16	15	-
Q	16	-
S	19	-

STEEL HOOKS

U.S.	Metric	U.K.
00	3.5	-
0	3.25	0
1	2.75	1
2	2.25	1.5
3	2.1	2
4	2	2.5
5	1.9	3
6	1.8	3.5
7	1.65	4
8	1.5	4.5
9	1.4	5
10	1.3	5.5
11	1.1	6
12	1	6.5
13	0.85	7
14	0.75	-

Meet the Designers

Susan Huxley, the author of *Crocheted Sweaters*, mastered the basics of crochet when she was five years old by making "the World's Longest Chain" during a cross-country car trip. Nurtured in a family of stitchers, she developed an appreciation for needle arts at an early age, and this passion inevitably merged with her publishing career. For almost two decades, Susan has worked as an author, editor, reporter, and crochet garment designer. She has been the editor of a national Canadian magazine called *Crafts Plus* and a senior editor of sewing books at Rodale Inc., and is now the owner of a contract publishing business. Visit her Web site, www.SewnTellStudio.com, to find out when she's speaking in your area and to learn new techniques, tips, and inspiration for crocheting, knitting, and garment sewing. A resident of Easton, Pennsylvania, Susan lives in a 200-year-old house with her husband, Bob Gerheart, and their standard poodle. Someday she hopes to spin the dog's trimmed fur into yarn that she can crochet.

Nancy Brown is a crochet pattern designer for the Skacel Collection, Inc. and also publishes pattern leaflets that are sold in yarn stores throughout the country. Her creations have appeared in national magazines, such as *McCall's Needlework* and *Crochet Fantasy*. Her *Hat Book*, available through ASN Publishing, is a bestseller. Nancy has served as executive vice president of the Crochet Guild of America (CGOA) and is the current CGOA trade show representative. She also conducts workshops for West Coast yarn stores and guilds, and teaches at national events, such as TNNA, CGOA, and Crochet Renaissance. This busy lady is the West Coast representative for the Skacel Collection, too, which she says gives her the best of both worlds because she can work with the newest yarns and interact with store owners, their customers, and yarn-industry representatives on a regular basis. Nancy lives on the Kitsap Peninsula of Washington, about an hour by ferry from Seattle. Her husband, Marco, doesn't crochet, but "has a brilliant design idea occasionally."

Tricia Crichton, a resident of Maplewood, New Jersey, is a member of the Crochet Guild of America (CGOA) and has been a crocheter since she learned to finger-chain as a preschooler. She now develops and sells crochet designs by using CAD drawings and spreadsheets to establish dimensions and increase patterns. Tricia says she's crocheted a little of everything, including slippers, sweaters, doilies, stuffed animals, rugs, garments, blankets, and hats. She works with a wide variety of hook sizes, from the giant size S to the tiny size 14 steel. She has also played with the use of alternative materials, such as single strands of sewing thread and wire. After majoring in French as an undergraduate and then studying cognitive anthropology in graduate school, Tricia decided that crocheting full-time would be more rewarding than pursuing an academic career.

Annabelle Dawson, who lives in Weston, Ontario, has been a custom knitter and crocheter since the 1960s. She has taught and worked in the design studios of Spinrite and Susanne Galat; designed for *Crafts Plus*; organized production for Mimi Bizjac, Wayne Box, and Wayne Clark; and produced custom designs for *Wind at My Back* and for several other television shows and films. Most of her designs now go to such companies as Shelridge Farm, Canaan, Belle Vallee, Woolen Acres, and Wood 'n Needles. Annabelle has also worked for Toronto yarn shops, Creative Crafts, Christine's Yarns, Village Yarns, and Clickity Wools; taught classes; and has led workshops for a wide variety of Canadian knitting guilds and collectives. At an age when most people retire, Annabelle is busier than ever—and insists that she doesn't plan to stop crocheting or knitting until the undertaker pries the needles from her hands. You can visit her at www.canknit.com/adawson.html.

Edie Eckman is a freelance designer with more than thirty years of knitting and crochet experience. Her patterns and articles have appeared in *Knitter's Magazine* and *Knitting Digest*, and in the publications of numerous yarn companies. The American School of Needlework has published her knitting and crochet pattern booklets, including *Crocheted Wardrobe for 18" Dolls* and *Crocheted Hats, Scarves and Mittens*. Edie, who lives in Waynesboro, Virginia, has been a technical advisor for a children's clothing designer, co-owned a retail yarn shop, taught both small groups and individuals at all skill levels, and custom knitted and sold items through local artisans' galleries. She is a member of the Professional Knitwear Designers Guild and the Crochet Guild of America (CGOA), and is a founding member and the ad hoc vice president and program director of the Shenandoah Spinners and Knitters Guild. A mother of two, Edie says she finds plenty of time for needlework while she waits for carpool pickups and during her children's swim-practice sessions.

Tosca J. Mark, who lives in Newmarket, Ontario, specializes in crochet and continental knitting. She is a CYCA (Craft Yarn Council of America) certified teacher; a member of the Canadian Knitwear Designers Association (CKDA); a professional member of the Crochet Guild of America (CGOA); and the owner of Yarns in Motion (www.YarnsInMotion.com), an Internet mail-order yarn company that also offers pattern design and instructional services. Tosca, who spent her childhood in Europe, learned to knit and crochet in school, and also inherited a lifelong love of knitting from her mother and grand-

mother. In 1964, when Tosca moved to Canada, she discovered commercial patterns and soon found herself using the design skills she'd learned from her mother to modify existing patterns and to create her own designs. In 1998, Tosca decided to combine her knitting and crochet skills, her love of fiber, and her academic background in mechanical engineering to establish Yarns in Motion.

Nancy Nehring is a nationally recognized author, teacher, and designer in the needle-arts field. She is the author of three books (*50 Heirloom Buttons to Make*, *The Lacy Knitting of Mary Schiffmann*, and *Ribbon Trims*), and her work has been published in numerous needle-art magazines, including *Threads* and *PieceWork*. Nancy has designed for DMC, Skacel, Donna Karan, and Better Homes and Gardens. She lectures and teaches locally, regionally, and nationally, and has lectured and led workshops at Crochet Renaissance, the Embroiderers' Guild of America annual Chain Link (the Crochet Guild of America's annual conference), and the Stitches seminar. Nancy lives in Sunnyvale, California, with her husband, three children, cat, bunny, cockatiel, chicken, and iguana. She's allergic to wool, so all of her designs are in cotton or synthetic yarns.

Nancy Rawlinson, who lives in Toronto, Ontario, is a veteran knitter, crocheter, and crafts designer. Under her label, Eat Sleep Knit (www.eatsleepknit.com), Nancy designs and produces retail knit and crochet patterns and kits, as well as knit and crocheted accessories, such as note cards,

bookmarks, and T-shirts. Nancy is a certified crochet instructor with the Craft Yarn Council of America (CYCA) and is completing the Master Hand Knitter program with The Knitting Guild of America. Her work has appeared in *Cast On*, the Knitting Guild of America's magazine, and she has self-published patterns for retail sale and for use in her classes. Nancy enjoys many handwork techniques, from basketry to beading. Through teaching workshops and creating her own designs, she enjoys exploring the use of unconventional materials and encouraging others to experience the tangible and intangible benefits of creativity.

Jane Snedden Peever, who has been a needle crafter since she was nine years old, has made everything from afghans to Barbie doll clothes. When she reached university age, she started to experiment with designing patterns. A few years later, Jane, who lives in Pembroke, Ontario, opened a store for personal needleworkers, where she sells her designs, patterns, and kits. After setting up an internet presence for her store, Jane's Wool Studio at www.janeswool.com, she decided to devote her energies exclusively to the Web site so that she'd have more time for designing and to spend with her children. Jane is still amazed by the number of people she meets and ideas she shares through the Internet.

"I've had a great deal of support from my family, especially my mom and dad, my husband, Todd, and my little girl, Tessa," Jane says. "They have always encouraged me to follow my dreams."

Acknowledgments and Resources

It's easy to assume that an author is the most important part of a book, but my role in *Crocheted Sweaters* is dwarfed by the creativity and experience of the many people who were part of this endeavor.

There's one group of publishing professionals that usually gets little glory, yet the people in it were responsible for turning my words into a beautiful book. I owe much to this book's team:

• Book packager Chris Rich (Asheville, NC) deserves special thanks for spearheading this project. With tact and humor,

she improved the instructions, pulled together the book team, and made sure that everything ran smoothly.

• Art director Theresa Gwynn, of Gwynn Designs (Flat Rock, NC), understood the special needs of crochet instructions, styled photography, and made sure that every page would inspire you.

• Photographer Brian Woodward brought the sweaters to life and captured the stitch details that we all love to see. Gry Karen Rick provided invaluable assistance with styling sweaters. Their business is

Woodward + Rick Photography, Inc., in Asheville, NC (www.wrphoto.com).

The photos in *Crocheted Sweaters* remind me of the excitement I felt every time another commissioned sweater arrived. Admiring the handwork of the talented designers was one of the highlights of writing this book. Thanks, ladies!

There's a saying in this business that anyone can write a book—the trick is getting it published. I'm thankful that Martingale & Company, in Woodinville, WA, believed in the vision that Chris Rich and I shared.

The company's personnel are wonderful. Thanks to publisher Jane Hamada, editorial director Mary Green, design and production manager Stan Green (one of my favorite designers), editorial project manager Tina Cook, technical editor Ursula Reikes, illustrator Laurel Strand, and copy editor Ellen Balstad.

For their yarns, swatches, and support, thanks to the following businesses and individuals: Creative Needle Studio (Hendersonville, NC); Earth Guild (Asheville, NC); Kraemer Yarn Shop (Nazareth, PA); Eleanor Love (Black Mountain, NC); Esther Moriarty (Marshall, NC); The Naked Sheep (Black Mountain, NC); Needle Art Studio (Emmaus, PA); Jane Sugawara (Hendersonville, NC); and Tangled Yarns (Bethlehem, PA).

For their expertise and advice, special thanks to Sandi Gainey (Allentown, PA); Robert Gerheart (Easton, PA); and Esther Moriarty (Marshall, NC).

Several people and associations were instrumental in getting out the word that I was calling for sweater-design submissions. Thanks to the Crochet Guild of America (www.crochet.org); the Knitting Guild of Canada; Vicki Chisam (www.groovycrochet.com); and Barbara Breiter (www.knitting.about.com).

I'm also very grateful to the yarn manufacturers and distributors whose generous support helped make this book possible. My special thanks go to Gayle Bunn at Patons/Bernat; Norah Gaughan at Reynolds/JCA; Deborah Harrison at Cascade Yarns, Inc.; Adina Klein at Lion Brand Yarn Company; Barry Klein at Trendsetter Yarns; John Little at Briggs & Little Woolen Mills Ltd.; Dick Power, Jr. and Uyvonne Bigham at Plymouth Yarn Company; Ingrid Skacel at Skacel Collection, Inc.; Peggy Wells at Brown Sheep Company; Inc.; Margery Winters at Berroco, Inc.; and the helpful staff at S.R. Kertzer Limited and Tahki Stacy Charles, Inc.

The yarns used in the sweaters in this book are manufactured and/or distributed by the companies listed on this page.

Bernat
PO Box 40
Listowel, ON
Canada
N4W 3H3
Web site: www.bernat.com

Berroco, Inc.
PO Box 367
Uxbridge, MA 01569
Tel: (508) 278-2527
E-mail: info@berroco.com
(Wholesale only)

Briggs & Little Woolen Mills Ltd.
3500 Route 635
Harvey, York County, NB
Canada
E6K 1J8
Tel: (800) 561-9276
Web site: www.briggsandlittle.com
E-mail: woolyarn@nb.sympatico.ca

Brown Sheep Company, Inc.
100662 County Road 16
Mitchell, NE 69357
Tel: (800) 826-9136
Web site: www.brownsheep.com
(Wholesale only)

Cascade Yarns Inc.
PO Box 58168
Tukwila, WA 98138
Tel: (800) 548-1048
Web site: www.cascadeyarns.com
(Wholesale only)

Coats & Clark (Red Heart Soft)
Consumer Services
PO Box 12229
Greenville, SC 29612
Tel: (800) 648-1479
Web site: www.coatsandclark.com

Lion Brand Yarn Company
34 West 15th Street
New York, NY 10011
Tel: (800) 258-9276
Web site: www.lionbrand.com

Patons
PO Box 40
Listowel, ON
Canada
N4W 3H3
Web site: www.patonsyarns.com

Plymouth Yarn Company
PO Box 28
Bristol, PA 19007
Tel: (215) 788-0459
Web site: www.plymouthyarn.com
E-mail: pyc@plymouthyarn.com
(Distributor, wholesale only, of Adriafil and Filatura Cervinia)

Reynolds/JCA
35 Scales Lane
Townsend, MA 01469
Tel: (978) 597-8794
(Wholesale only)

Skacel Collection, Inc.
PO Box 88110
Seattle, WA 98138
Tel: (800) 255-1278
Web site: www.skacelknitting.com
E-mail: info@skacelknitting.com
(Wholesale only)

S.R. Kertzer Limited
105a Winges Road
Woodbridge, ON
Canada
L4L 6C2
Tel: (800) 263-2354
Web site: www.kertzer.com
E-mail: info@kertzer.com
(Distributor, in Canada only, of Super 10)

Tahki Stacy Charles, Inc.
8000 Cooper Ave.
Bldg. 1
Glendale, NY 11385
Tel: (800) 338-9276
Web site: www.tahki.com
(Distributor, wholesale only, of Filatura Di Crosa)

Trendsetter Yarns
16742 Stagg St.
Suite 104
Van Nuys, CA 91406
Tel: (818) 780-5497
E-mail: trndstr@aol.com
(Wholesale only)